William Gordon Stables

Rota Vitae

The cyclist's guide to health and rational enjoyment

William Gordon Stables

Rota Vitae
The cyclist's guide to health and rational enjoyment

ISBN/EAN: 9783337065522

Printed in Europe, USA, Canada, Australia, Japan

Cover: Foto ©Lupo / pixelio.de

More available books at **www.hansebooks.com**

A GLIMPSE OF DERWENTWATER.

ROTA VITÆ:

THE CYCLIST'S GUIDE TO HEALTH & RATIONAL ENJOYMENT.

BY

GORDON STABLES, C.M., M.D., R.N.,

AUTHOR OF

"Medical Life in the Navy,"   "Turkish and other Baths,"
"Tea: the Drink of Pleasure and of Health,"
"Health upon Wheels," &c., &c.

LONDON:
ILIFFE & SON, 3, ST. BRIDE STREET, E.C.
1889.

CONTENTS.

	PAGE
CHAPTER I.—Introductory—My Friend Russell and I	9
CHAPTER II.—A Morning at Grace Church Priory—Hints about Healthful Rational Touring	14
CHAPTER III.—Sunny Memories of a Summer's Ramble	22
CHAPTER IV.—East Northumbria—Belford and the Regions round Wooler — Chillingham — Alnwick — Rothbury — Brenckburn—A Tale of Romance—The Holy Isle	29
CHAPTER V.—Berwick and Surroundings—Bonnie Ayton—Tweedmouth and Spittal — Norham Castle — Twizel Castle — Flodden — Kelso — Melrose — Dryburgh — St. Abb's Head	38
CHAPTER VI.—Haddington and Round it—Cockburnspath—The Caves—Pressmannan Loch—North Berwick—Dirleton Castle	45
CHAPTER VII.—Touring in Scotland—New Routes Recommended—Touring in England—Districts to go to for Health and Pleasure's sakes	53
CHAPTER VIII.—Physiological Facts about Food, Alcohol, Ærated Drinks, Smoking, and Tea	61
CHAPTER IX.—On Exercise—Winter Riding—Pure Air—Common Sense about Sleep—The Bath—Mountain Dew *versus* Whiskey	69
CHAPTER X.—Facts about Physic	77
CHAPTER XI.—Advice to Ladies—Weakly People and Invalids—Ailments for which Cycling is Recommended	82
CHAPTER XII.—"Do" or "Don't," or Suicide made easy	92
CHAPTER XIII.—Hobbies and Health—Recreation—On Growing Old—Pastime Studies for Cyclists	98
XIV.—Fishing: A Pastime for the Summer Holiday—Concluding Advice	107

ADVERTISEMENTS.

THE
FAIRY MEDICINE CHEST,
OR
CYCLISTS' AND TOURISTS' *VADE MECUM.*

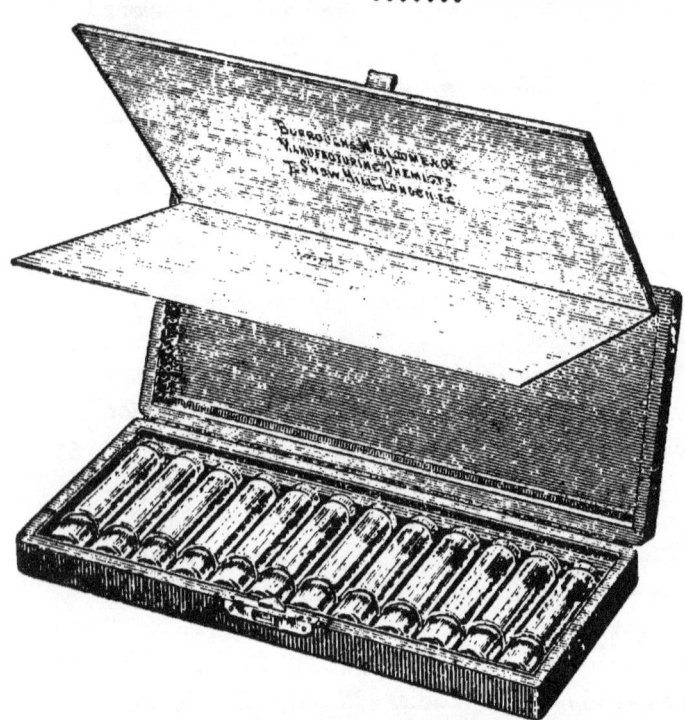

THIS beautiful little Case is exactly what it professes to be— a Cyclists' and Tourists' *Vade Mecum.* It has been got *by* a cyclist *for* cyclists, by a traveller for travellers, and no pains or thought have been spared to make it complete. Not only is it *com*plete, but *re*plete with every drug and medical and surgical appliance likely to be needed in an emergency by the tourist. It has the best tonics, the best aperients and diaphoretics, the safest and most certain remedies for the alleviation of pain and cure of colds, and the only safe narcotic. Every accident or ailment likely to occur on the road has been provided against, and the whole Case is so small as to go easily into the cyclist's bag, or the tourist's dressing-case.

A complete Guide for the use of this portable Pharmacopœia is also included, and a few small but perfect surgical appliances and instruments.

PRICE, FREE BY POST, 12/6.

Apply to Messrs. BURROUGHS. WELLCOME & CO., Snow Hill, London, the Makers; or to Dr. GORDON STABLES, R.N., Twyford, Berks, the Inventor, who will, if desired, add special remedies for special cases.

ROTA VITÆ.

CHAPTER I.

INTRODUCTORY.—My Friend Russell and I.

WE met at Northallerton, my City friend and I. It was in the dusk of a beautiful summer's evening, and in a lane near the town. The air was redolent of newly-mown hay, and the hedgerows on each side of the path were starred over with wild roses, crimson, pink and white.

I was enjoying my usual evening stroll, quietly meditating on anything, everything, nothing, for I was pleasantly—tired. Physiologically speaking, the blood, owing to the wholesome and not over-fatiguing exercise I had been indulging in during the day, was determined away from the brain. It was in the limbs, the lungs, anywhere you please, but not sensibly in the brain. My brow was cool, the cephalic capillaries were not overgorged, no danger of them losing their resiliency or elasticity. By-and-bye, gloaming would deepen into night, and I would retire to my couch to enjoy that delicious dreamless slumber, which is only vouchsafed to the just and to those who ride in reason.

Someone on the other side of the way—someone whom I thought I ought to know—arrayed in a light, loose mackintosh, and pacing slowly up and downas if doing "sentry-go." That tall, spare figure, with a trifle of a stoop in the shoulders—it must be—it *is*—my friend Russell, whom I last saw at an accountant's desk in a court off Mincing Lane.

A minute afterwards we were walking slowly townwards, arm-in-arm, talking about old times and new times and times to come—these latter were to be good times.

Russell's room at his hotel looked out towards the garden. The window was open to the top, but, singular to say, there was a bright bit of fire in the grate.

"Looks snug, you know," he said, answering my enquiring look. "Well, what'll you drink? You found me just cooling myself down after a long ride. It's best not to sit down damp, don't you think so?˙ But what will you drink—soda and B.? Champagne, if you like."

"I don't set up for a saint, Russell," I replied, "but I do not care to have anything more to-night."

"Nonsense, man."

"I've just dined—or call it supper. If I ingest liquid now, it will not only weaken the gastric juices, but prevent the stomachic walls from having full play on my *cibum*."

"Oh, *don't!*" cried Russell.

"I *will*," I said, determinedly. "The stomach cannot act on the *cibum*, or food, till the fluid is absorbed, and digestion would thus be hindered—result, a restless night. Again, the nerve-cells of my cerebrum——"

Russell clapped his fingers in his ears, but I went doggedly on—"Of my cerebrum are now at rest, and the capillaries partially empty. If I take a stimulant now I re-fill the capillaries and start the cells into a state of motion and ferment again; hence will come bad dreams, or weary, worrying dreams. The same will occur to the blood-vessels and cells of the cerebellum, which, as you know, Russell, presides over voluntary motion, and restlessness will be the penalty. I'll kick and flounder all night, and awake unrefreshed."

" Have a cigar, then."

" Ah! that is more in reason, and accords with the best received doctrines——"

" Look here!" roared Russell, " if there is any more physiology I'm off out."

" All right; sit still."

" What have you been doing?"

" Tricycling and caravaning to and fro since first of May. And you?"

" Oh, I'm doing a record. I've been to John-o'-Groat's, and am on my return journey. I did seventy miles since eight this morning. Let me see, now—I left London on——"

" Stop!" I cried, " I hate records as much as you do physiology."

" And forgive me, old man," I continued, " if I tell you that you are doing, and have been doing, a very foolish thing. Straight up from the desk you start, with flesh as flabby as an old mare's. Out of condition, in fact, not over well—no city desk-slave is—you go madly at it. Your heart muscles must be stretched, and you're thinner."

" I'm harder," said he.

" I doubt it. Your cheeks are more hollow, skin

more sallow; you've lost some of the cushion of fat that ought to lie behind each eye, and your legs——"

"Well, what about my legs?"

"They are no thicker than a lamp-glass, and not half so well shaped. They put me in mind of pea-sticks; a touch would frac——"

"Doctor!" cried Russell, jumping up and taking a few strides across the floor, "if I didn't know you well, I'd feel inclined to——"

"Throw me over the window, eh? I doubt if you could."

Russell sat down laughing.

"No use being angry," he said.

"Not a bit. Well, now, tell me how have you enjoyed yourself. Seen much of the scenery? Visited many old ruins? Been on the steeple-tops of many fine old churches? Had many adventures and many incidents by the way? Been studying botany at all? Geology? Had time to look at and admire the splendid trees, the wealth of wild flowers that bedeck the sward, and the glorious hues of summer's mantle spread over the hedgerows, the trailing roses, the sheets of white bryonia, the honeysuckle, yellow, brown, and red, and the purple of the creeping vetch? Of course you had a day or two among the crimson heather, and a moonlight sail on many a bonnie loch? No? Then what on earth have you done, Russell?"

"A record. I left London——"

"The ultimate ramifications of the nerves of organic——"

"For goodness sake!" cried Russell.

"For goodness sake yourself. If you give me records, I'll return you physiology. There!"

"Well, let it be a bargain," said my friend. "No talking of records, and no talking Greek. Now tell us all your adventures," he added.

"Not to-night. But to-morrow let us start early, very early, and breakfast on the road *al fresco*. I can manage it. We'll run to Mount Grace Priory, and there, among
            Woods and wilds, and melancholy gloom,
I'll tell you something about my cruise."

"All right," said Russell, "and bother my record. I'll end it here, I think. I'll take it easier after this. You've frightened me almost with your grim physiology, your cerebrums, and capillaries, and hollow cheeks, and cushioned eyes, and all such fearful talk. A tankard of bitter, please, waiter.

"A tankard of buttermilk would be better for you. Good night."

"Good night. I don't believe I'll sleep a wink."

"Good night. I know I will."

CHAPTER II.

A Morning at Grace Church Priory.—Hints about Healthful Rational Touring.

AN eight miles ride on a lovely summer's morning, through a charming country, no matter how rough the road is, can hardly be called tiring, and is bound to give a cyclist an appetite. Not that my friend Russell and I left Northallerton without a bite and sup. The bite was merely a luncheon biscuit, the sup a glass of new milk.

No one, let me say parenthetically, should take much exercise in the morning on an empty stomach; it does more harm than good, for it weakens the system. Moreover, one is thus more likely to catch infection of any kind. Here is a case in point: I walked four miles once before breakfast to a house where scarlet fever was raging. Seven days afterwards I myself was down with the same, and it was six weeks before I got out of doors again.

"Is milk and rum a good thing," I have been asked, "to take first thing in the morning?" Here is my answer. "To one glass of milk add two tablespoonfuls of rum, then —— pour it into the slop-pail. It will not hurt the slop-pail a bit, but it will hurt you, if you drink it. Get up and have a cold or tepid bath instead."

Two new-laid eggs each, with a rasher of delicious bacon, bread (rolls) and country butter galore, with fragrant tea, that was the breakfast Russell and I discussed on a hill above grand old Grace Priory, and near to a ruin called the Lady's Chapel.

"Why is it, or was it, called Lady's Chapel, I wonder?" I asked, dreamily, as we lay on the sward. The day was far too glorious for deep conversation.

"Why shouldn't it be?" was the reply. "Here, have a cigarette."

"Thanks."

"I daresay," continued Russell, lighting up, "the ladies of the Priory came to pray here."

"Ladies, my dear sir! Listen while I read you a sentence or two out of my wee guide-book":

The ruins are situated in a romantic and secluded position at the western foot of the Arncliffe Woods, which rise behind the walls from the eastward, so that during the winter months the sun would have to rise high in the heavens before it illuminated, by its cheerful light, the lonely monastery. This gloom may have been suitable to the Carthusian monks, who were modelled on the order of St. Benedict, but of far greater strictness and severity. The habits of the Carthusians were entirely white, except a plaited black cloak; they wore a hair cloth next the skin, and walked in their grounds once a week. Their bed was of straw, with a coarse cloth upon it; their covering a sheepskin or a piece of coarse cloth; their clothing two hair cloths, two cowls, two pairs of hose, cloak, &c., all being of the coarsest texture. They were not allowed to eat flesh, and fasted on bread and water every Friday. At their meals each monk was obliged to eat alone in his cell, except on Sundays and feast-days, when they dined together in the Refectory in silence. Women were on no account permitted to enter the precincts of the Priory.

"But," I said, "it is Our Lady's Chapel, and not the Lady's Chapel, though often called so."

It was indeed a beautiful day. From our vantage

ground we had a view of an undulating and well-wooded country, that was worth riding eighty miles instead of eight to view.

Clouds floated across the sun's disc every now and then, and cooled his otherwise fierce rays. High above them there must have been some wind, but where we lay hardly was there air enough to bend the feathery grasses. Silence almost unbroken was everywhere. The only bird we could hear singing was the yellow-hammer. Though not one of the earliest songsters of spring, this bright, happy fellow continues his sweet little lilt all through the months of autumn.

Peet! peet! peet! peet! peet! peet! pee-ee! thus it goes from morn till dewy eve, the first notes short and rapid, the last a sweetness long drawn out. Trowbridge's words come to my memory as I listen, and I cannot help repeating them to Russell, who, strange to say, loves poetry far better than he does physiology:

> Long-drawn and clear its closes were—
> As if the hand of Music, through
> The sombre robe of silence drew
> A thread of golden gossamer;
> So pure a flute the fairy blew.
> Like beggared princes of the wood,
> In silver rays the birches stood;
> The hemlocks, lordly counsellors,
> Were dumb; the sturdy servitors,
> In beechen jackets patched and grey,
> Seemed waiting spellbound all the day
> That low entrancing note to hear—
> Pe-wee! pe-wee—pe-wee—pee-eer!

When tired of roaming about the grand old Priory, which, by the way, has a history far too long for me to

GRACE CHURCH PRIORY.   17

give here, we hied us away to the woods. Our object was to find the wishing well.* Not that I wished to wish, or that Russell wished to wish, but we would see the well, and drink of its waters, if possible.

We met a little ragged boy. He seemed to want to avoid us, but the sight of sixpence, produced with a smile, was a sufficient lure. Perhaps he had been after no good; but he served our turn, and brought us to the old stone well. Its waters once supplied the Priory.

But lady cyclists should not neglect to visit this well. For why? Only for this reason. You throw a bent pin into the water, and *wish*. You must not let anyone know what you are wishing. You must wish in silence, without even permitting your lips to move, and your wish is certain to be fulfilled. So it is said, at least.

We arrived "home" in time for an early dinner, and Russell confessed he had really enjoyed himself, and spent a most pleasant and happy day.

We dined all by ourselves in a quiet little room. Given a well-cooked, well-served dinner, soup that is soup—*i.e.*, not made from the chop bones, and bits of steak or kidney left on plates, as much of the soup presented to you in confectioners' shops is. Given salmon that swam in the limpid river but the day before, an *entrée* and a joint, a salad and a modicum of wine. Let the silver be bright, the table-linen like snow, and the crystal shine like diamonds—what more is needed to complete the picture, except a couple of cyclists pleasantly, joyfully hungry?

---

*St. John's Well.

And now, dear reader, my friend Russell must drop out of the book, with one remark—I have made him a convert to my doctrine of cycling for health and rational enjoyment.

I do not think he will make any more mad records. Land's End may know him no more. He may never again be seen speeding across the Grampians *en route* for John-o'-Groat's.

But in many a sylvan fairy nook he may still be met during his summer holiday, or jogging along o'er lonely wolds in Yorkshire, or among crimson heath-clad hills in Wales, or fishing in lochs and tarns in green Caledonia, and wherever you find Russell, you may take my word for it his tricycle will not be far away.

And what is this doctrine of mine? you may ask. I am going to spread it out before the reader all through this little book, and though it is one that may not be adopted by everybody, I feel convinced it will be by not a few.

From one article of mine in a summer number of " The Girl's Own Paper " I cull the following as *à propos* —it may be read with some degree of interest by lady cyclists.

I am talking about my annual holiday, when I say:

I study my guide before I start, then I pack my portmanteau, and ride off to the nearest railway station. The train conveys me to my holiday home, and after that I have only to look out for quiet lodgings. No hotels for me, thank you.

Once established in my quarters, I set about enjoying myself in a rational way. I want no companions except my dog, and a favourite author or two, and my *vade mecum* is my fishing-rod.

I never go fishing for sake of making a record, or booking the number of trouts I catch; if the fish are hungry, and willing to be caught, I have sport; if they are shy, owing to the brightness of the day, or lowness of the water, I put up my rod, and sit by the banks of the stream and read and dream day-dreams. When tired of reading, I put my book in my bag, remount my tricycle, which is always at hand, and ride off to visit some old castle with a story to it, or some battle-field, which—my imagination being a healthy one—I can very easily re-people with the ghosts of dead-and-gone heroes, who, at my bidding, fight the battle o'er again for my especial benefit.

But I have one other way of enjoying myself in my holiday home. I get up early on a fine morning, mount my iron horse, and start for a long ride, without knowing in the least where the road will lead to, or where it will land me. To this plan I am indebted for many strange adventures, and for much genuine enjoyment.

My faithful companion and guard has hitherto been my noble champion Newfoundland, "Hurricane Bob." Bob, by-the-bye, has only one home, and that is wherever his master happens to be.

When we once start on a journey of discovery, then, if we can see along one road for a couple of miles or so, we turn our backs upon it; if another goes away down through a green shady wood, and, after a few hundred yards, suddenly disappears, it suits us.

"Come along, Bob," I say, "we'll see where this road goes to, anyhow."

"All right," Bob replies, "it is sure to lead us somewhere."

And it always does. Down by the banks of brawling streamlets, perhaps, deep into gloomy pine forests, with fences of green turf riddled with rabbit holes, the owners themselves probably peeping out, with their ears on end, then drawing cautiously in again; while, farther into the wood, leverets may be at play on a carpet of last year's withered pine-needles. Past old-fashioned water-mills, their broad wheels revolving with steady, drowsy hum, their buckets very black, and the spray and foam that dashes over them from the mill-head looking snow-white in contrast. Past cosy farm steadings, past fields where sleek cows are feeding, and shiny-skinned horses, who have nothing to do but nibble each other's shoulders, because it is their holiday time—

early harvest. Past rolling fields of ripening grain, down through "bosky" glens, pretty enough and wild enough to be the residence of fairies, where giant ferns grow, brown stalked, with palm-like fronds, and where crimson foxgloves ("dead men's bells") nod in the sunny air.

Through these "bosky" glens and up again on to broad lone moorlands, with on one side glimpses of the river, broad and shallow as it goes dancing over a bed of pebbles, or deep and narrow in pools where great salmon love to sleep, and where the birch-clad braes that rise precipitously from the water were reflected as in a mirror, with, on the other, perhaps, the summit of a distant mountain showing darkling over the crimson heather-moor in the foreground.

Tired at last, Bob and I perhaps find ourselves inside the walls of a ruined castle. Ah! could those crumbling walls, so old and grey, over which the ivy trails, on top of which even broom grows tall and wiry—could they but speak, what a tale they could tell us!

The grass that grows on the floor of the old hall is very soft, and here we cook and spread our banquet. What does it consist of? Why, crisp oat-cakes with the sweetest of butter, new-laid eggs which we have purchased by the way at a little cottage, and fragrant coffee. Good enough for a king; good enough, at all events, for Bob and me.

I do not know what Bob lies down to think about. I have "Ivanhoe," and it is not very long before the knights of old step right out of the book and throng around me in that old castle hall. Then I suppose the book itself falls out of my hand, as the next thing I am conscious of is the flapping of wings right above me. The wild pigeons who have been from home all day eating bilberries (*Scottice*—blaeberries) have come home to roost. I start up, and so does Bob. The great dog shakes himself to show he is quite ready for the road.

Yes, and so am I. But as soon as mounted, the question of "Whither away?" presents itself. Well, it is too late now to dream of reaching home to-night. A bivouac in the castle among the bats and owls would be wearisome in the extreme; and as we have passed no village on our way, the probability is that if we continue to go on we will come to one. Besides, as Bob said "the road will be sure to lead us somewhere." So on we go.

The sun has gone down some time. It is a lovely night, though, with a strangely beautiful after-glow in the east. A lady might be able to give a name to the colour of the sky betwixt the dark blue of the upper dome in which the stars are already twinkling merrily, and the clear pale yellow along the horizon. No gentleman could, though, unless an artist, and even a lady would have to fall back upon some of those fashionable tints or shades that they give to dresses, the very names of which make us poor men folks open our eyes with wonder. On we go, and the colour fades out of the east, and a nearly full moon rises slowly up over the woods.

On we go, and on and on, but the road really seems to have given up all idea of leading anywhere in particular.

What joy now, to come to some cosy little roadside inn, just as we least expect it, or from the brow of some hill to see the lights of a village twinkling in the distance!

This is a plan of touring which, though I cannot recommend it to ladies, would be found very pleasurable for gentlemen of an imaginative and probably adventure-loving turn of mind.

CHAPTER III.

Sunny Memories of a Summer's Ramble.

THIS ramble of mine took place last summer, and was not only a very extended one, but in many ways unique.

As, however, it was of a description but very few of my readers can have it in their power to imitate, I will be very brief in my description thereof.

The one peculiar feature about it was this: I not only had my cycle, but took with me all along my hotel! My hotel was my now well-known caravan, "The Wanderer."

She is quite a house upon wheels, a splendid saloon drawn by two powerful horses, and fitted up with every comfort and luxury a gipsy of the first water could wish for.

My servants were my coachman and my valet. The former fed and slept at the inn at which the horses were stabled, the valet was my cook and secretary, and slept at night in the after-cabin of the caravan.

The actual ground covered by "The Wanderer" from the first week in May to the middle of October was over 1,200 miles. Either myself or valet were constantly in the saddle, and counting the numerous detours made and the many side-places visited by me, down narrow roads where "The Wanderer" could not be taken, the tricycle must have done about 2,500 miles, but I have no exact record, and never meant to make one.

I had at first intended taking two cycles—my beautiful " Salvo " and the " Ranelagh Club," but an unfortunate accident to the former decided me in starting with the " Ranelagh" only.

I may say for it, once for all, that probably no machine was ever put more sternly to the test on all kinds of roads, and in all kinds of weathers, and, certainly, the "Ranelagh" stood it well. The tyres are cut, and we had one or two spills—two, I think. The marvel is we had no more, for down steep hills we used not to run but to fly. She is as good as ever to-day, and I used her this winter* almost every day. An easy saddle, quick motion, capital propelling power, and good, reliable brake and steering gear make the " Ranelagh " a most desirable machine.

After doing the east side of Berks, and a portion of Surrey and Hants, "The Wanderer" started on her journey due north with her little busy satellite, the " Ranelagh Club."

We took it easy. My object was thorough enjoyment. The longest day " The Wanderer " had was under 30 miles.

We always had a mid-day halt to bait, to cook and feed, and rest; then on again.

We usually managed matters so that we avoided arriving at night at big towns, for we soon learned that stabling here was more expensive, and the noise and bustle was far from agreeable to anyone enamoured of a gipsy life.

---

* 1885—1886.

I much preferred getting to some little wayside inn towards sundown, where, after "The Wanderer" was drawn into a meadow, and the horses were stabled and seen to, perfect quiet reigned around us, broken only by the evening song of birds and those country sounds so dear and so soothing to the ear of a lover of nature.

We provisioned on the road, buying meat and groceries at the shops; but milk, fresh butter, eggs, fowls, and vegetables at the houses of farmers or cottagers.

Our cooking apparatus is a largish Rippingille range, which stands in the after-cabin, and takes up but little room. On hot days this range can be taken out and placed under the caravan, and so the saloon is kept cool.

My route lay along the river Thames westward as far as Wallingford; then right away north and east through the chief towns and counties, not catching a sight of the sea until shortly after leaving Gosforth, on the other side of Newcastle.

We hugged the east shore all the way to Edinburgh, from which ancient city we branched off to Glasgow, etc., and thence made our way to Perth, and so on over the Grampians to Inverness. The roads over the mountains were very bad, and at one part, being run into by a frightened horse, the whole expedition was nearly hurled over a precipice 500 feet high, which would have brought my romantic cruise to an ugly conclusion.

As a rule, the roads are better for cycling in Scotland than in England. The English go *over* their hills. Our Scotch hills are too high, so we wind round them. But in many mountainous districts, especially if it be wet, cycling is far from a pleasant pastime.

The southern portion of my cruise was a very enjoyable one. It was now autumn, and the woods were looking their best, though we missed the wild flowers by the wayside, and the birds had ceased to sing. My route now lay from London to Brighton, and all along the South Coast, round Southampton, through Lyndhurst to Lymington, and back north to Berkshire. If the reader has never been to the New Forest, he or she has a treat which I trust is to come.

At Inverness, as at every town I went to, I was boarded by a reporter, and the following excerpt from a newspaper may not be devoid of interest to those who care to peruse it:—

A GENTLEMAN GIPSY.

Many of our readers are aware that Dr. Gordon Stables, R.N., a gentleman well known as an author and journalist, is on his way to Inverness, travelling in his own caravan, and he has given the following amusing account of his trip to a contemporary:—

Yes, I may say I have had some little experience of a gentleman gipsy's life and its ups and downs. I started cruising about the end of April this year, and left South Berkshire for my long journey on 18th of June. I had no idea how far I might travel, so much depends on one's horses; mine have proved invaluable. Being a Scot, it was but natural my nose should point northwards, as the needle points to the pole. I followed my nose. The roads They are far better in Scotland than England, where they are often very narrow and shockingly badly kept. Even in Oxfordshire and Berks we had some frightful hills, needing the iron shoe for down and the roller for up. "The Wanderer" weighs nearly two tons, and if she took charge on a steep hill, she might roll backwards and come to grief. The worst hill we encountered was at Alnwick, where nothing but the timely assistance of the mob prevented an ugly smash. Hills are heavy in Durham, and all over Northumberland. The roads are naturally dangerous for a heavy waggon in some parts of the

Scottish Highlands. I am not likely to forget the Pass of Killiecrankie, while some parts of the path to Dalwhinnie look as if they had been well harrowed. It is harrowing to think of. N.B. —The mountain air I am breathing is to blame for the pun.

"The Wanderer" was built for me by the Bristol Waggon Company, and from my own plans. Her roof length, from stem to stern, is 19ft. 6in., and her internal breadth 6ft. There is an after-compartment with folding doors, which is kitchen, pantry, and my valet's room. The coachman sleeps where the horses are, and often the broad dickie, with canvas round it, is his lot.

Cooking is done in a Rippingille range. That range has been a blessing. We can cook anything—fish, flesh, fowl or pheasant, and in a neat and cleanly way. Cleanliness and regularity are with us next to godliness. There is no system in an ordinary gipsy van; everything is lubberly and higgledy-piggledy. Ours is all system; hence there are comfort and piece. There are awnings for the roof and sides, and a tent behind to cook and wash up under. It is also my bath tent. The bath is simply a bucket of cold water and a big sponge.

Foes to our comfort are mud and dust, but we defy both, and a green turf cut from the roadside and laid beneath the after-steps makes a most convenient mat. We start of a morning as soon as we can get cleaned up. There are many little things to be done that take up time, so, although we are never in bed after six, it is generally eight before the steps are shipped and horses started. We do from five to seven miles an hour, but I halt very frequently to take notes and study nature; then there is a long mid-day halt to bait and cook, so that we are generally nine hours on the road every day. Bar Sunday? Yes, I have never travelled on Sunday yet, and hope I never shall. Being fresh from the drudgery of journalistic duties, I found the exercise fatiguing at first, but have hardened to it, and sleep better at night than ever I did in my life. The sofa by day is my bed by night, lockers beneath containing the blankets and pillows. The shutters are drawn on by nine or ten o'clock, and by eleven all is still. The armoury consists of a revolver, my navy sword, a civil tongue, and "Hurricane Bob," my champion Newfoundland. He is a grand guard.

The only time we were molested was at Deddington, a village of savages in England. I was mistaken for General Booth. In a narrow street "Hurricane Bob" stemmed a howling mob till the caravan drove on into Dr. Turner's grounds. I have bivouacked on lonely roads in the Black Country among the roughest miners and roughest folks of all sorts, and never had any bother. Quite the reverse, for those same black sheep brought me little gifts of new potatoes and gooseberries, and their children brought me flowers. I have often forgathered with real gipsies. They are always civil, though they laughingly hail me as brother. I have had very few accidents, and they were but trifling—a bent axle, for instance, or a slight collide, stuck in a meadow at Chryston and smashed harness, but twenty or thirty Chryston miners came to the rescue, and did what three great horses could not accomplish.

I have a "Ranelagh Club" tricycle, which is a splendid roadster and invaluable to me. My valet rides on ahead as pilot, and often I take little rambles across country on it, and always in the evening I ride on to secure accommodation for the horse and a place in which to bivouack.

Now, everyone to his taste, and I to mine, but I consider caravan travelling the most enjoyable of any. The railway is not to be compared to it. In a train you are always on the dead level, you have no time to see anything, the brain is tired with the eternal roar of the wheels, with the grind and gride, while you are smothered by sulphurous fumes in tunnels, and half choked with dust in the open. In a train you may be hungry, and cannot get aught to eat; thirsty, and open your mouth at a station only to swallow poison; and if you enter into conversation for a couple of hours, perhaps you have a splitting headache next day.

River yachting is nice enough, but here again you are on the level, and see absolutely nothing; while at night there are the blighting dews and fogs, on which float rheumatism, dyspepsia, and bronchitis itself. Besides, I know that people who travel in river boats drink a lot. That is plain English. A caravanite doesn't need to drink to keep up his spirits. The fresh, pure air of heaven is the best stimulant in existence, and this he has in plenty, and has nothing to pay for it either. And he is nearly always hungry; he can eat four good meals a day, and can do with a bit of bread and cheese between whiles. Plain food is all he needs, and this he can purchase on the road. Eggs, potatoes, and green vegetables from cottagers; milk, butter, and fowls from the farmer; and game anywhere.

The constant change of scene, the ever-varying incidents, strange faces, strange people, and strange sights, little adventures, and the absence of all care, combine to make a caravanite's existence a most enjoyable one indeed.

CHAPTER IV.

EAST NORTHUMBRIA.—BELFORD AND THE REGIONS AROUND.—
WOOLER. — CHILLINGHAM. — ALNWICK. — ROTHBURY. —
BRENCKBURN.—A TALE OF ROMANCE.—THE HOLY ISLE.

THE Cycling tourist can hardly do better than make Belford his headquarters for a time, while he visits the delightful scenery of East Northumbria. He will find capital quarters, and if my experience is anything to go by, cheap, at the Blue Bell Hotel there.

Northumberland is, altogether, a most romantic and beautiful country, and its history ought to be well read up before visiting it. The coast line, with its marvellous isles and castles, possesses a charm for me that I would try in vain to describe, or even to analyse.

Who, while wandering or riding near the shore, does not remember the bold heroic lines of Sir Walter Scott in describing the voyage of the " Holy Maids " to St. Cuthbert's Isle :

> The breeze that swept away the smoke
> Round Norham Castle rolled,
> When all the loud artillery spoke,
> With lightning-flash and thunder-stroke,
> As Marmion left the hold.
> It curled not Tweed alone, that breeze,
> For, far upon the Northumbrian seas
> It freshly blew, and strong,

When, from high Whitby's cloistered pile,
Bound to St. Cuthbert's holy isle,
It bore a barque along.
On the deck, in chair of state,
The Abbess of St. Hilda placed,
With five fair nuns, the galley graced.
  * * * *

And now the vessel skirts the strand
Of mountainous Northumberland ;
Towns, towers, and hills successive rise,
And catch the nuns' delighted eyes.
Monk-Wearmouth soon behind them lay,
And Tynemouth's priory and bay ;
They marked, amid her trees, the hall
Of lofty Seaton-Delaval ;
They saw the Blythe and Wansbeck floods
Rush to the sea through sounding woods ;
They passed the tower of Widdrington,
Mother of many a valiant son ;
At Coquet-isle their beads they tell
To the good saint who owned the cell ;
Then did the Aln attention claim,
And Warkworth, proud of Percy's name ;
And next, they crossed themselves to hear
The whitening breakers sound so near,
Where, boiling through the rocks they roar
On Dunstanborough's cavern'd shore ;
Thy tower, proud Ramborough, marked they there,
King Ida's castle, huge and square,
From its tall rock look grimly down,
And on the swelling ocean frown ;
Then from the coast they bore away,
And reached the Holy Island's bay.

Says another writer :

On the iron-bound coast the sea sweeps roaring in upon the wall of rocks, and rises high in spray and foam, ancient ruins frown from the shapeless rocks, and here and there in some gap in the stern barrier the smoke from a fisher-cottage relieves the sombre desolation of the scene. Here the breeze blows, pure and fresh, from the very sources of the winds. Here the past assumes a distinct importance of its own. Among the little towns, and about the old churches and border towers, the footsteps of time have not been effaced by a crowd of events. Whatever deeds were done here lang syne, little has happened since to disturb their memory.

Amid so much striking and romantic scenery, in a country with so ancient and so warlike a history, it is difficult to advise the reader where to go or what to visit first.

If you glance at the map, you will see that the town of Wooler lies within easy distance of Belford to the west. Riding southwards about two miles, you will find the cross-road leading to the right direct for Wooler. This will give you an opportunity which should not be missed of visiting Chillingham Castle, and seeing the beautiful wild cattle.

The colour of these animals is a pure white, the ears inside and about a third of the outside, from the tips downwards, are red. The horns are very fine—white usually, with black tips, and the muzzles are black. Some of the bulls have a raised mane. These bulls had best be avoided, they are often dangerous.

If you now ride on you will soon come to Wooler, and will be delighted with the scenery, the Cheviot Hills, and the wood and water everywhere around. The church of Wooler is pretty, and there are cairns and entrenchments to be visited, besides the hill of Humbledon Heugh, which please climb; you will not repent it.

From Belford you will find your way south to Alnwick, through charming scenery. On the hill-top about, as far as I can remember, two and a-half miles from Alnwick, on a knoll on the right you will notice a round tower. Do not forget to climb this knoll, as one of the finest views in England may be had from it on a fine day.

There is so much to be seen about the ancient and pretty town of Alnwick (pronounced Annick) that you will do well to sojourn here for at least one day and night.

Alnwick is the county town of Northumberland, and is very ancient. There was a guide to Alnwick published some years ago, and still to be had at the shops, price sixpence. It is very complete, and no one who visits the romantic old place should be without it. Space, or rather the lack of it, forbids me doing more than merely mentioning the names of the chief places of interest here.

1. Alnwick Castle, the seat of the Percies, and by far and away the noblest pile of building in the North.
2. The Gardens.
3. Alnwick Abbey.
4. The Cemetery.
5. Holm Priory.
6. The Parks and Pleasure Grounds.
7. St. Michael's Church.
8. St. Mary's Church.
9. St. Paul's Church.

The freemen of the borough of Alnwick are now enrolled with very little ceremony, but formerly the custom of going through the well used to be in vogue. The immersion used to take place on the 25th of March.

So graphically does Davison, in his "History of Alnwick," describe the curious ceremony that I cannot refrain from quoting him :

ALNWICK. 33

Early in the morning of St. Mark's Day, the houses of the new freemen are distinguished by a holly tree planted before each door, as a signal for their friends to assemble and make merry with them. About eight o'clock, the candidates for the franchise being mounted on horseback, and armed with swords, assemble in the Market Place, where they are joined by the chamberlains and bailiff of His Grace the Duke of Northumberland, attended by two men with halberts. The young freemen being arrayed in order, with music playing before them, and accompanied by a numerous cavalcade, march to the west end of the town, where they deliver their swords. They then proceed, under the guidance of the moorgrieves, through a part of their domain, till they reach the ceremonial well, where their friends await their arrival, provided with refreshments. The well is situated near a place called Freemen's Hill, and about four miles south-west of the town. It is a dirty stagnant pool nearly twenty yards in length, and is suffered to run out during the rest of the year; but those who are entrusted with this matter take care that it shall lose none of its depth or size at the approach of St. Mark's Day. The young freemen having arrived at the well, immediately prepare for immersion; and after divesting themselves of their proper garments, they are soon equipped in a white dress and a cap ornamented with ribbons, the sons of the oldest freemen having the honour of taking the first leap; and being arranged accordingly, when the signal is given, they plunge into the ceremonial well, and scramble through the noisome pool with great labour and difficulty, and after being well drenched and nearly suffocated with mud, they are assisted out of the puddle at the further end in a rueful condition, and afford a truly ludicrous and amusing scene to the spectators. After this aquatic performance, they speedily resume their former dresses, and taking a dram to dissipate the vapours after the legalised plunge, they remount their horses and proceed to perambulate the remainder of their large common, of which they are become free by this achievement. When arrived about two miles from the town, they arrange themselves in order, and to prove their equestrian abilities, set off with great spirit and speed over bogs, ditches, whins, rocks, and rugged declivities, till they arrive at Rotten Row Tower, the foremost claiming the honour of what is termed "winning the boundaries," and of being entitled to the temporary triumphs of the day. Having completed the circuit, the young freemen, with sword in hand, enter the town in triumph, preceded by music, and accompanied by a large concourse of people in carriages, on horseback, and on foot, who have been enjoying the pleasures of the day. Leaving the streets the new freemen and the other equestrians enter the castle, where they are liberally regaled, and drink the healths of the lord and lady of the manor. The new-created burgesses then proceed as a body to their respective houses, and around the holly tree drink a glass with each other. After this they proceed to the Market Place, where they close the ceremony over an enlivening bowl of punch. They then retire to their respective homes to enjoy the pleasures of social festivity, which prevail to the end of the following day.

Round and about Alnwick are many places of note worth spending a day at.

Felton, on the river Coquet, for instance, a most romantically situated little village in a glen, about ten miles from Alnwick, south. Brainshaugh, with its curious old church. Rothbury, twelve miles from Alnwick, on the Coquet, among beautiful hills and woods. Rothbury Church is a great centre of attraction to tourists. Brenckburn, with its beautiful old priory. And last, but not least, Warkworth, distance from Alnwick about eight and a-half miles. It is the castle that attracts everyone. It is a fine old pile, on high ground, by the river Coquet. The view from here is very grand. The village itself is very small, numbering considerably under a thousand souls.

The castle is probably eleven hundreds of years old. Its story is far too long to tell in my pages. Get it and read it. I may mention, however, a fact that will already be known to many of my readers, that Shakespeare lays a scene in one of his plays here. It is truly a magnificent ruin, standing on nearly five acres and a-half of ground, and nearly surrounded by the Coquet. The donjon keep especially will please the visitor.

Having wandered over the ruins, viewed everything, and mused, as you cannot help doing, on the days of this castle's glory and grandeur, now gone for ever, you will leave by the postern gate, and find your way to a walk that goes along by the river side. This will guide you to a landing, from which you will be ferried over to the Hermitage.

> The Armytage belded within a rocke of stone
> Within my park at Warkworthe.

The whole place is really hewn out of the rock, chapel, altar, confessional, dormitory and all.

This must have been a somewhat gloomy abode for the hermit. He is surely now in a better world. That he had sins which he wished to expiate on this earth might be supposed from the inscription over the doorway—"*Fuerunt mihi lacrymæ meæ panies nocte ae die*," which translated literally would run thus: "Tears have been my bread by night and by day." There had been at one time an upper room, but it is ruined. Altogether the place is exceedingly interesting.

> A little lowly hermitage it was,
>   Down in a dale, hard by a forest's side;
> Far from resort of people that did pass,
>   Or travelled to and fro a little wyde.
> There was a holy chapell edifyde,
>   Wherein the hermit duelly went to say
> His holy things each morn and eventyde;
>   Thereby a crystall stream did gently play,
> Which from a sacred fountain welled alway.

A lady cyclist who has been reading this MS. during a temporary absence from my study takes objection to my allusion to the expiation of sins mentioned above.

"He loved," she says; "his lady died, life had no more charms for him, and the tears he shed were to her memory, the prayers he said and the blameless life he led were to ensure his meeting her in the realms above."

So be it.

Anyhow, not far from the altar is a monument which I feel sure will interest my fair readers who visit at this romantic shrine. The image of a lady recumbent, beside her a knight kneeling in an attitude of grief, on her left an angel, at her feet a dog.

I'm glad there is a dog : *

. . . . man's best friend,
The only creature constant to the end.

Bishop Percy, in his beautiful ballad, weaves the story of the Hemitage round this monument. Whether he is right or not in supposing the knight to be a |Bertram and the lady-love a Widdrington matters very little indeed :

>Young Bertram loved a beauteous maid,
>As fair as fair might be,
>The dew-drop on the lily's cheek,
>Was not so fair as she.
>Fair Widdrington, the maiden's name,
>Yon tower's her dwelling-place ;
>Her sire an old Northumbrian chief
>Devoted to thy race.
>   *   *   *   *   *   *
>The bold Sir Bertram now no more
>Impetuous, haughty wild:
>But poor and humble Benedict,
>Now lowly, patient, mild.

---

* It is certainly a dog of no particular breed, but Percy must be wrong in supposing it is a bull (part of the arms of the Widdringtons). A bull-dog, if you please, but not a bull.

My lands I give to feed the poor,
And sacred altars raise;
And here a lonely anchorite
I came to end my days.

This sweet sequestered vale I choose,
These rocks and hanging grove:
For oft beside that murmuring stream
My love was wont to rove.

My noble friend approved my choice:
This blest retreat he gave:
And here I carved her beauteous form,
And scoop'd this holy cave.

Full fifty winters all forlorn,
My life I've lingered here,
And daily o'er this sculptur'd saint
I drop the pensive tear.

Bamborough Castle is but five miles distant rom Belford. It is a place of great strength and antiquity, boldly standing over the sea on a precipitous cliff nearly 200 feet in height.

The Holy Isle, or Lindisfarne, with its church and priory and castle, will occupy a whole day in visiting, and if the history of the place has been read beforehand, it will indeed be a day well spent.

There are many other places round Belford worthy of mention, did space permit, notably the Farne Islands.

I may mention, for the benefit of my invalid readers, that residence can be had cheaply on the Holy Island itself, and that it would be difficult to find a place bettei suited to brace up the nerves of those who may have been weakened in constitution by hard work or worry, or by both combined.

CHAPTER V.

BERWICK AND SURROUNDINGS.—BONNIE AYTON.—TWEEDMOUTH AND SPITTAL.—UP THE RIVER.—NORHAM CASTLE.—TWIZEL CASTLE.—FLODDEN.— KELSO.— MELROSE.— DRYBURGH.— ABBOTSFORD.—ST. ABB'S HEAD.

WHEN I rode across the old bridge over the Tweed and down with a rush—for the town end of it is very steep—into Berwick, I said to myself—

This is my own, my native land.

It matters nothing to me that the place has English laws. I care not that the Berwickites themselves say they belong to neither country, and that they are free and independent. To my way of thinking the silvery Tweed is the boundary line here 'twixt Merrie England and "the land of the mountain and the flood."

Ah! but for centuries before the happy union, Berwick was a terrible bone of contention, and fearful were the fights, and dreadful the massacres that used to occur periodically in its streets or around it.

Did not Edward I. besiege the ancient place in the 13th century, and finally take it by strategy and assault? Yonder, from the grass-grown remains of the old wall, rises the ruins of the Bell Tower, from which the tocsin was wont to sound. It was near here that Edward made his furious assault with the whole strength of his army. It is sad to think that the thirty brave Flemings who defended the Red Hall till the last were finally burned in the ruins, and that the inhabitants to the number of 8,000 were ruthlessly butchered in the streets and in their houses!

From that day onwards Berwick was continually changing hands and owners, and the whole history of the place a black and bloody one, though it is eminently readable.

The cyclist will do well to make Berwick his headquarters during a holiday. He will find the people kind, hospitable, and chatty, and the place itself well worthy of rambling through again and again. If, however, he be of my way of thinking, he will prefer viewing the remains of ruins they call the Castle, and the old walls, to sauntering among public buildings. The pier is worthy of a few visits, especially by moonlight, or in the gloaming of a summer's evening; along the seashore, too, is a delightful walk, and, if fond of geology, one that will well repay the tourist. He will come to caves worn out by wave-action in the sandstone.

A pleasant ride on good roads due north, with the cliffs and blue sea not far off on the right, will bring you to Lamberton Toll, where you enter Scotland proper. Only a cottage or two at each side of the road, but here the Border marriages used to be made by priests, so the place is not devoid of interest. There is said to be a signboard on one house informing people that this is " The House for Border Marriages."

I sought after this sign, but found it not.

On the left, about half a mile or less from the road, is Lamberton Farm, and the ruins of the old church where the sister of Henry VII. was married (by proxy) to James IV.—the happiest marriage that ever was celebrated for Britain, for from this union did not the union of Scotland and England itself arise? Farther still to the west is the Witch's Knowe and the site of a Danish camp.

Round southward by Halidon you will find many places of interest, and you can return to Berwick by another road leading from Canty's Bridge over the Whitadder (pronounced Whitider).

If you pass on through the toll and away north you will find the country, though at first only a series of green bare knolls, very charming and picturesque, and about eight miles from Berwick you cross a bridge in view of a pretty modern-built castle, and enter the lovely village of Ayton on the Eye, which seems to go wimpling round it as if loth to leave the bonnie place.

What a spot for a honeymoon! Wonder if honeymooners do come here? The words of the old song came into my head as I crossed the bridge, and I sang, as I rode into the town—

> In a sweet little village,
>   By the banks of a stream,
> Where poets love to wander,
>   And where music seems to dream;
> In the little shady lanes,
>   Long before I was a man,
> Did I whisper words of love
>   To my little Mary Ann.

Go to the Temperance Hotel; say I sent you, if so minded. The honest landlord will not forget "The Wanderer," and you will have something good to eat and rest for the night, should you feel inclined to stay for fishing.

No cyclist should leave Berwick without taking a boat trip up the Tweed. The banks and the river bridges are thus so much better seen. Choose a fine day, or it will be labour and money lost.

I myself can see no beauty about Tweedmouth and Spittal. The view, however, from the hill-top about two miles from the former village is very beautiful. You will have to walk a greater part of the way up. What of that? on returning you do not require to touch treadle until you come to the old bridge of Tweed. They tell me that at Spittal there is a chalybeate spa of great value in ailments of the blood. I have no knowledge of it further than hearsay; my invalid readers may, if so minded, find it out for themselves.

There used to be a wide moorland south of Spittal and Tweedmouth, which was the scene of the brave Grizel Cochrane's encounter with the postman, when, dressed in male attire, she met, dismounted, and robbed him of the bags containing dispatches ordering her father's execution. Sir John Cochrane was afterwards pardoned.

Now, there is no necessity for even a cyclist being for ever on wheels. Certainly, if it is a choice between a horse-conveyance—be it dogcart or coach—and his "tri.," he will choose the latter, but if a pleasant cruise can be made in a boat, he will probably make it by way of change. Get a good oarsman, then, one who knows the river well, and all its history and traditions, catch the tide at its early flow, and hie up the river to the Chain Bridge or to Horncliffe. I do not mean to waste my precious space in an attempt to describe all you will see, but I do say, emphatically, that if favoured with a fine day, your enjoyment will be very great.

See the lovely glen called the Dean, and then ask your way to Norham Castle. It is a ruin, and a most romantic one, 700 years old. Read the history of it before you visit it.

Not only will you thoroughly enjoy your visit to the noble old castle, but the scenery all around here you will find enchanting. I know of no adjective that describes it better than that word "enchanting." There is a fine old Norman church at Norham, which is certainly worthy of a few minutes' admiration.

I am not sure but that some of my cycling friends, having once seen Norham village, may feel inclined to make it their headquarters instead of Berwick itself—so quiet, retired, and healthy is the place.

About four miles to the westward, and south of Norham, is the splendid Castle of Twizel. It stands on an elbow of rock, a wildly picturesque situation, by the river. It is here the Till joins the Tweed, and not far from the castle is the old bridge that crosses the Till, and by which the English army crossed the Till on their way to the fatal field of Flodden. It is a bridge of but one wide span, but nothing could be more lovely than the appearance of the wooded banks of the slow-winding Till here on a summer's day.

Flodden field will repay one for a visit thereto. While

viewing the battle-ground a good deal will have to be left to your own imagination—it is not now what it was. If an Englishman, you may exult as you think how on this very spot the flower of the Scottish army was laid low; if a man, you will feel nothing but admiration for the brave nobles who rallied round their king, and died, sword in hand, fighting for him.

Twenty-three miles from Berwick is the town of Kelso. As the roads are very good it may easily be done in a day; you may start in the early morning and sleep again at Berwick that night. But the invalid or weakly person must not fatigue himself.

At Coldstream, just ten miles from Kelso, a pretty village with good views, the cyclist can stop and lunch, or at least refresh.

Hardly will you find prettier scenery anywhere than that about the beautiful town of Kelso. It stands on the Tweed, near to and opposite the junction of that river with the Teviot. The principal objects of interest, not to mention the river itself and all the sweet scenery, is the Bridge, the grand old romantic Abbey, the Palace of Floors, not far off, with its beautiful garden and grounds, and the ruins of Hume Castle.

If inclined to see a bit of gipsy life, take a run to Yetholm, a place now of summer resort, owing to the purity of its air and fishing.

You will probably be inclined to rest the night at Kelso, and go on next day to Melrose, distant about fourteen miles, which is too well known to need more than mention, and on thence to Dryburgh Abbey, a magnificent ruin. Do not forget that Scott's tomb is in St. Mary's Isle, and also those of his wife, his son, and son-in-law.

Near the Abbey is Dryburgh Mansion.

Abbotsford lies about three miles west of Melrose. There are very many other places of interest in this charming district, all of which the cycling tourist will easily find out from guide-books.

Let me earnestly entreat of him not to be in a hurry, for hurry is destruction to happiness and health. Let him not spend all his time on the cycle either; but rather do whatever is most convenient; short journeys by rail may help him, the cycle may accompany him. Little boat cruises on the Tweed or Teviot will add to his enjoyment, but above all let him climb hills, and view the scenery therefrom. Nothing will give greater pleasure than this.

* * * *

I must now suppose we are back again at Berwick. Find your way north to St. Abb's Head. Great indeed will be your reward. A wilder scene than the shores here present, especially on a stormy day, it would be difficult to conceive. The hills, the beetling crags, the dark wave-washed rocks and giant boulders, the screaming flocks of sea-birds, the monastery ruins, the lighthouse, and Fast Castle, all combine to form scenery that once visited can never be forgotten.

The villages of Coldingham and Eyemouth will delight you; in the latter little fishing town and seaport you will be certain to see something new.

CHAPTER VI.

Haddington and Round it.—Cockburnspath.—The Caves.—Pressmannan Loch.—North Berwick.—Dirleton Castle.

HADDINGTON is one of the quaintest and most old-fashioned towns in all broad Scotland. Indeed, it has quite a character of its own, a character that pervades its houses, its streets, and even its inhabitants. Although my stay here was brief, I bore away with me nothing but the kindliest recollections of the hospitality with which I had been received.

Where did I read—or have I been dreaming—that there is a very large admixture of Irish blood among the good folks of Haddington Well, never mind, the Irish are Celts, and I—a Celt myself—have a very soft side towards dear old ill-used Erin.

Out upon those who say, in their ignorance, that nothing honest or genuine can come out of Ireland ; even if I did not know the Irish people, I would judge them by the melodies of their native country. Next to old Scotland itself, Erin is the land of poetry and song. I shall take my fiddle in my hand, dear Saxon reader, and play you some of their grand old sorrow-laden lilts, and if I do not melt you, why you can have no soul.

Well, in Haddington you shall find several good hotels. You cannot have a better than "The George."

You will find it well worth while to walk through the streets—not to ride, for they are very rough—and examine the old houses.

You will visit the Abbey and Church, and poor Mrs. Carlyle's grave, past which the river flows placidly on. You would scarce think, to see it, that ever it came down in spate.* But it does, and once, in 1358, it destroyed houses and villages on its banks, and threatened even the destruction of the Abbey itself.

But the whole history of Haddington is well worthy of being perused.

The health or pleasure-seeker might do well to make this fine old town his headquarters for a month. Let him sleep there at night, at all events, but every day, wet or dry, let him be on the move.

I say wet or dry advisedly, for the plan I recommend of taking an outing on the cycle, or spending the holiday on wheels, carries with it no fatigue. The gentleman, or lady either, who cannot do a short twenty or five-and-twenty miles on a summer's day, even should it be blowing, has no business to be riding at all.

You can always dine out, either at the town you visit or at some small wayside inn, even if you do not adopt my own plan of carrying the capabilities of cooking your dinner *al fresco*.

At small inns one does not get a great set-out, but if it be only new-laid eggs, bacon, and tea, why the appetite you bring along with you will make it seem a dinner fit for a king.

---

*Spate.—A quick, heavy flood, caused by rains swellin the tributaries and streams roaring down from the hillsides.

Everywhere you go around Haddington, you will be charmed with the character and beauty of the scenery, and its great variety.

Inland, are there not grand old hills and wild woodlands, lonely straths and glens, and splendid sheets of water? Is there not, too, the finest tree scenery that exists anywhere in Scotland? Yes! and the very wild flowers and hedgerows themselves, would repay one for all the toil incurred in rattling over somewhat stony roads, and climbing lofty braelands. Then, towards the east, you come in sight of the sea itself—the ever-beautiful, ever-changing sea. Go farther east, go to the coast itself, and you will find yourself among such rock scenery, as can hardly be beaten, except by that in Skye or the Orkneys. When tired wandering on the shore, and, if a naturalist, studying and admiring the thousand-and-one strange objects around you, why you may go and hob-nob with some of the fisher-folks—male or female, take your choice—they will amuse—ay, and mayhap instruct you, while some of the oldest of them will tell you tales of the old smuggling days, and life in the caves that will beat anything you ever read in books.

At the office of the *Haddingtonshire Courier* is published a handy sort of guide-book to the places of interest within a very easy day's run—back and fore—of the town. It is more than a guide-book, for it really brings the scenery most vividly before the mind's eye.

The tourist would do well to get this book, which I think costs but a shilling, and before he starts on a little outing read up the history of the place he is about to visit.

It is good to have a book of this kind. Just one example—I could give a hundred. On my way to Cockburnspath, and near to a lonely and beautifully-wooded glen, I came suddenly upon the ruins of an old redstone castle, on the edge of a wood. Of course, I dismounted, and I went and sat down on a stone, and I wondered much where I might be, and what was the history of the pretty old and lonesome ruin. But I had no guide-book, the walls refused to speak, and the croodling wild pigeons were far too busy making love to have anything to say to me. I could only call upon my own imagination to assist me.

Nor did I know at the time that I was close to the romantic dell called Pease Dene.

This was a treat I missed, but the cyclist who makes Haddington his headquarters must be more fortunate. The sylvan beauty and the grandeur of the glen once seen, so they tell me, will be remembered for ever.

The Pease burn rises among the Lammermoor Hills, and here runs at the bottom of a deep gorge that is spanned by a bridge so lofty and beautiful that, seen from beneath, it appears to hang in the air, and one cannot help wondering whether it was not the fairies themselves who were the architects.

But this locality has an interest for the lovers of history quite apart from its romance and beauty, for here the English Independents, under Cromwell, and the Scottish Covenanters met in deadly fray. How fierce the tulzie was—how fearful the fight! But the better generalship gained the day. The Scotch were beaten back, leaving hills and glens strewn with the flower of their army. No use wishing now-a-days that it had been otherwise, or that the proud invader, the destroyer of noble churches and despoiler of cities and towns had been hurled into the sea. History is history, and we cannot alter it.

Descending from the sublime to the useful: you can get a snack of something good to eat, if you tell them to prepare it, at the inn of Cockburnspath. If you should stay here all night, you will not forget to visit the sea-shore and the caves. Those caves have a history, too, they were connected with the troublesome times of auld lang syne, and, later still, they came in remarkably handy for bold smugglers, who, before the days of smart revenue cutters, made use of them as temporary store-houses when running a cargo on shore.

How lovely the sea looks on a summer's day from the hills around here! How enchanting the woods! How wild! How quiet! You will be inclined to live and linger among scenery such as this, book in hand, perhaps, on a bank of wild thyme and bluebells, and if you do notice some blue-coated bicyclist, with red perspiring face and dusty *tout ensemble*, speeding past on his way to John-o'-Groat's, how you will pity him!

Farther west is the romantic Dunglass Dene, which you will visit without fail. Says Scott:

>   The cliffs here rear their haughty head
>   High o'er the river's darksome bed;
>   Here trees to every crevice clung,
>   And o'er the dell their branches hung;
>   And there, all splintered and uneven,

> The shivered rocks ascend to heaven;
> Oft, too, the ivy swathed their breast,
> And wreathed their garland round their crest;
> Or from the spires bade loosely flare
> Its tendrils in the summer air.

I do not think I ever enjoyed a visit to any place more than to Pressmannan Loch, but it was from Dunbar I went. I do not remember what was the distance. On a lovely day in August, with sea and woods and hills and hedges all aglow in the sunlight, what has distance to do with one's pleasure? The roads were fairly good, however, though there was one long ascent just before getting over the hill and down to the loch. But the view from that hill I am never likely to forget, nor the solitary beauty of the quiet winding lake with its braeland of trees that look like green clouds.

Pressmannan Loch is about eight miles from Haddington, and there is a gradual ascent along the base of the hill of Trepain. You pass through the pretty village of Whittingham, and through a lovely country to Stenton village. The road will need some walking, however, but what odds—you are sure to be happy. Had I met a party coming to Pressmannan from Haddington while I was coming from Dunbar, it is at Stenton where we would have forgathered, and then gone up the long hill I have already mentioned together, and so on to the loch.

I do not intend to describe the scenery. Go, see it for yourself, dear reader, I'm not a guide-book, but I can assure you of one happy, quiet day in your chequered career if you only visit Pressmannan Loch.

Not far from here, only Dunbar way, is the estate of

Biel, its splendid park and grand old terraced gardens—all open to the public through the kindness of Miss Hamilton. Biel is an earthly paradise. To say more were needless.

You can visit this and go on then to Tyningham, the seat of the noble house of Haddington. See the woods and forests of Tyningham, see the sylvan loveliness of the Wilderness, and see, if possible, the Haddington Gardens—if you go on the right day you can—do all this, and you will have something to think about in the winter months when home again in the city, and you will thank me for sending you thither.

Close by Haddington is Lennoxlove Castle. It has a history which you had better read up; it has a garden and grounds which you will never regret having visited.

By the way, though, there are some places in Scotland, and in East Lothian in particular, which the families who reside there do not care to allow the public to visit in their absence. I have found it a good plan to find out the name of some servant left behind, say a housekeeper, and giving my name at the lodge gate, tell the porter I am going to visit her. I hope I may be forgiven for suggesting the adoption of this plan to my worthy readers; if they are more honest than I, they will shrink aghast from it—if not, they will not. The sin is not a great one.

Among other castles too numerous to name within an easy ride of Haddington is Crichtoun. It is but a ruin, but well worthy of a visit—a noble ruin. A tall and lofty square pile of masonry, which has stood the assaults of many a foe, and the wear and tear of time—that enemy before which every created thing must fall at last—for many hundreds of years. It stands on high ground over the Tyne, which is here but small indeed. The castle has a wonderfully romantic history which takes us back hundreds and hundreds of years.

A visit should be paid to North Berwick, which will be very much enjoyed. Two miles or little over from this town, passing along by the sea, you come to the pretty wee village of Dirleton, where at the inn you can order the necessaries of life while you visit the old castle, with its battlements and tower. This ruin is very ancient, dating back at least to 1200. It was once the home of the Ruthvens. Patrick, Earl of Ruthven, and surnamed the Awful, was one of, if not the chief murderer of David Rizzio. Dirleton Castle has a black, black history; if the old ivy-clad walls could only speak they would whisper a tale that would cause one's blood to run cold.

Hailes Castle is about half an hour's journey by cycle from Haddington.

Here it is said Bothwell and Queen Mary rested a night when on their way from Dunbar to Carberry Hill. It is but a ruin, though a noble one, now, but the scenery all around the place is pretty and romantic, and quite enough to please the most fastidious.

CHAPTER VII.

TOURING IN SCOTLAND.—NEW ROUTES RECOMMENDED.—TOURING IN ENGLAND.—DISTRICTS TO GO TO FOR HEALTH AND PLEASURE'S SAKES.

MY reasons for dwelling more upon the scenery of Scotland than England in this "Guide to Health" are five-fold. First—and I am not ashamed to confess it—I am a Scot, and I dearly love

> The land of the rock and the wild wood,
> The hill and the forest and proud swelling wave,
> The land where bliss smiled on the days of my childhood,
> The land of the free, the home of the brave.

Secondly, I recommend cyclists to tour in Scotland because the scenery is so truly grand, and has a character about it that is nowhere else to be found in Great Britain. What says Byron?—

> Yet, Caledonia, dear are thy mountains,
> Round their white summits though elements war,
> Though cataracts foam 'stead of smooth flowing fountains,
> I sigh for the valley of dark Loch-na-gar.
>
> England, thy beauties are tame and domestic
> To one who has roved on the mountains afar.
> Oh! for the crags that are wild and majestic,
> The steep frowning glories of dark Loch-na-gar.

Thirdly, a residence in a mountain land is ever so much more bracing than dwelling on the plains. Fourthly, to enjoy a perfect holiday the tourist can hardly be too far away from home. And fifthly, Scotland is rich in historical interest, while its geology, its botany—I might almost say its flora and fauna—are, or will be, quite new to the English reader.

I must take this opportunity, however, of saying that I am very much disappointed at the way English, American, and most foreign tourists set about "doing" Scotland, as they call it. Their plan is most irrational, most silly. Writing recently in a London magazine, I make the following remarks on this subject. They are quite *à propos:*—

Wherever I go—and there is no corner of the British Islands, from St. Heliers to Lerwick, that I have not visited and lived in—it is the same.

It may be to some midland county of England, some sweet, green, tree-clad, bee-haunted, bird-haunted shire—

>Where poets love to wander,
>Where music seems to dream.

It may be away in wilder Wales, in the rolling plains of Yorks, in the Vale of Avoca, in the Trossachs, in the Straths of Dee, or in romantic Skye itself, the people you meet are nearly all of a type—if British, and especially if English.

I need not give a plurality of examples to prove what I assert; let one suffice. I travelled not long ago in the "mail coach," a rattling well-horsed four-in-hand, from the town of B——, in the highlands of Scotland, to the enchanting wee sea-side village of A——. The coach was crowded inside and out. We passed through one of the most romantic and charming mountainous districts in the country. All historical too. Hardly a mile of those purple moorlands, not a braeland, not a rock that had not once been a battlefield.

Was there anyone in that coach, think you, knew anything at all about the country or its history? If there was, he gave no sign either by look or by word. The conversation among the various groups in this four-in-hand was exciting enough, because there was the bracing breeze blowing in our faces, and exhilarating mind and body; but it was empty and commonplace, precisely the same as you would hear in towns.

NEW ROUTES RECOMMENDED. 55

But they admired the scenery? you will say. Nay, I'm sure they hardly looked at anything, so much enraptured were they with their own discussions and small talk. In fact, they were "doing" Scotland, and they were glad when the coach drew up at the village hotel door.

And every one of those tourists expected, and got, quite as good a dinner, and of much the same style, as they would have sat down to in an hotel in town. They were crowded enough for sleeping accommodation, but they would prefer a berth on a sofa or a table, or the hearthrug, to going to quiet private lodgings, as did I and a friend who was with me, where we had plain homely fare—but the best of that—and quiet and comfort, and where we could read and think.

Now, there are many districts in Scotland, where it is as rare a circumstance to meet with a tourist in any shape or form as to see a ghost. More rare, indeed, if we are to put any faith in the superstitions of the country. While, for example, the Deeside Highlands is well frequented, the charming country around the upper reaches of the Don is almost entirely neglected.

Now, cyclists can do both. Having journeyed all over the wild, romantic land, in the centre of which our beloved Queen has made her home, let him return to Aberdeen, and start thence up the Don. He will find there a charming country, not quite so wild as Braemar, but even more historical, for it is studded with old castles, and every castle has its story. Fishing, too, will be more easily obtained, and sometimes—if the cyclist knows the secret of making friends—shooting also.

Moreover, I have this to say about the less frequented districts of Scotland—living is therein cheap. I could mention scores of delightfully quiet little villages which, if cyclists cared to make headquarters of, they could live in comfortable country lodgings for a mere nominal sum per week.

The east coast of Aberdeenshire, though somewhat bare and woodless, should be more visited than it is. Peterhead and Fraserburgh might be the headquarters— good hotels and cheap lodging-houses. The Buchan district might then be investigated, with its ruined castles and its wondrous rocks and bullers. Many a happy dreamful summer's day might be spent by the seashore, or out in boats, on the beautiful blue waters of the German Ocean.

Not only here, but all round the coasts of Banff and Moray and Nairn, most excellent sea-fishing may be had for nothing except the hire of the boat and your tackle, which is simple enough in all conscience.

I want, before going any farther in this chapter, to impress upon my reader the fact that the whole eastern shores of Scotland are not half so well known to tourists as they ought to be, and that if a cyclist will only make choice of any district between Kirkcaldy and Peterhead, and spend a month in it, he will enjoy a treat quite new to him, and lay up a store of health that will stand him in need till the holiday season comes round again.

Inverness is one of the centres I must recommend, but here again I would advise the cyclist not to be too fond of following beaten tracks. Let him "do" all the sights and see all the lions, by all means ; let him go down by the Caledonian Canal to Foyers, or even as far as Fort Augustus, and back by the northern banks of Loch Ness ; let him go to Culloden and everywhere else about, then,

NEW ROUTES RECOMMENDED. 57

having done so, if he has the stamina, is not quite an invalid, and possesses a good strong cycle, let him take a tour backwards to the south and east across the Grampians. He will by this means gain experiences of magnificent mountain, loch and forest scenery that will be new to him, unless, indeed, he be a veritable gipsy.

I would advise anyone wishing to thoroughly brace up his nervous and muscular system, after, perhaps, a winter's sickness, or, what is just as bad, a winter's toil and worry, to sojourn a fortnight at Dalwhinnie Hotel; he will find a home there in every sense of the word, amid Nature's wildest grandeur, plenty of boating and fishing, and any amount of hill-climbing, and I believe, if he or she happens to mention my name—"The Wanderer"—the bill will not be an overwhelming one. It would not be so, at any rate, and this gives me the chance of saying that it is a very great mistake to imagine that the Scotch hotel tariff is in any way higher than the English. But there are exceptions, and before making up one's mind to sojourn for a season at a hotel, it is always best to ask the prices.

Helmsdale is a little village of about 1,000 inhabitants, that may be noticed on even a Bradshaw's map. It lies on the east coast of the Northern Highlands, half-way betwixt Dornoch and Wick. It is a capital centre for the district—one of the wildest and most lonesome in Scotland—from Tain to Dunnet Head, and from the German Ocean to the wild Atlantic.

Skye I can highly recommend to the cycling invalid or pleasure-seeker. There is no grander scenery any-

D

where in the world, and there is assuredly no place more bracing. When I lived there I had only one fault to find with the island—I got too often hungry. I used to have three or four meals a day regularly enough, and never objected to bread and honey or a new-laid egg beaten up in milk between whiles. Glasgow and Edinburgh are two famous centres for cyclists. Edinburgh even an invalid may live in with profit to his health, but I can hardly say the same of Glasgow.

Not that I have not the very greatest respect for both the city and its citizens. The latter, indeed, are, in my opinion, as a class, far better educated than Londoners, and possessed of all the cuteness and business habits of genuine New Yorkers.

Have not Glasgow's sons fought on every battle-field in every land under the sun? Do they not make money, both at home and abroad? Do they not make it honestly? Are not Glasgow's merchants called princes, and their homes palaces? Are not the public buildings in Glasgow the finest on the face of the globe?

Never mind about the smoke, spring dust, and November fogs, but look at her parks on a sunny day. I have sojourned in New York, and duly admired the sylvan beauties of the New Park, but give me Queen's Park, Glasgow, and give me Kelvin Grove.

If we call the cities of Scotland—they are not many —sisters, the daughters of
   Scotland, my auld respected mither,
then Edinburgh must be looked upon as the eldest, the proudest, and the noblest. She may well be excused for

NEW ROUTES RECOMMENDED.

keeping somewhat aloof from all the rest, standing on her dignity, as it were. She is the sister who holds on high the honour and glory of the family. Glasgow, on the other hand, is the sister who has married wealth. She is Madame Commerce. Lady Edina does not condescend to boast about her rich sister. That were *infra dig.*, but nevertheless she is secretly proud of her, and smiles in her own sleeve when she hears her styled the second city of the Empire.

Aberdeen is a younger sister, who, in a mild way, apes the manners of both Glasgow and Edina, and is somewhat jealous of the former.

Elgin is the old maid sister.

Dunblane is dreadfully down in the world, if ever she was up. She prides herself principally on the ruins of her old cathedral and the fine old song, "Jessie, the Flower of Dunblane." She is the silly sister.

St. Andrew's, again, is well liked by all the sisters. Scotia may well be proud of this daughter. Though not wealthy, she keeps up her ancient dignity, and has never brought disgrace on the family.

But to return to Glasgow. With the best water in the world, it is not a healthy city, and, having seen the sights in it, the touring cyclist had better take up his quarters at some village near it, and thence do all the charming scenery of the Clyde and a great portion of the Southern Highlands.

Dumfries should be the centre for the land of Burns. Perth, Dundee, Oban, St. Andrew's and Ayr may be other centres.

Coming south now to England, I must permit the cyclist himself to choose his own headquarters. I shall merely mention the most healthy and interesting districts.

1. The Lake Country.
2. The Yorkshire District (most bracing and interesting).
3. The Peak District of Derbyshire.
4. The Midland District.
5. The East Coasts.
6. North Wales (centre, probably Bala).
7. South Wales.
8. South Devon.
9. South Cornwall.
10. Jersey (St. Heliers).
11. Orkney (very healthy and bracing).
12. Shetland.

In both the last-named districts riding will be found practical, but boating excursions will rival the tricycle. Fishing and shooting, and walking among the moorlands and hills, combine to render a holiday in either the Orkneys or Shetland Islands a most enjoyable one.

Both at Kirkwall and Lerwick fairly good hotels are to be found, and respectable lodgings, while living is as cheap as anyone could desire.

CHAPTER VIII.

Physiological Facts about Food, Alcohol, Aerated Drinks, Smoking, and Tea.

IN this and the following chapter I wish briefly to state a few plain truths connected with the sciences of hygiene and therapeutics, and I shall do so in the simplest and least technical language I can command, so that he or she who runs may read.

I do not consider that verbiage is necessary to a proper understanding of the facts of physiology, nor is simplicity of diction opposed to a correct comprehension of the doctrines of any science.

To me, indeed, it has always seemed that the lecture system at our medical schools is a great mistake. The amount of useless language and needless harangue in these professional speeches, are painful to listen to by any student who possesses the slightest spark of common sense. Very few lecturers have acquired the art of condensation in their rhetoric. They hide the precious light of truth under a bushel, and the student has to lift the bushel to find it; they hide their needles in haystacks, and their grains of solid fact in gallons of chaff. It would be far better for the medical student, and far better for his future patients, if half the time he spends in stuffy lecture rooms were spent in the fields, with cricket ball or bat in hand, or in the woods with Nature, or along the roads among the hedgerows astride of a well-made cycle.

Let me ask any student who may read these lines, to add up the sum total of all he has ever learned from lectures, and tell me if I am not right in saying that he could have learned ten times more from books in one-tenth of the time.

When a professor has anything new to say, let him say it; even then it would be better far to print it, and distribute his knowledge in leaflets to his class: his students would very quickly skim off the froth and master the facts. Then demonstration in the dead-house, and experience gained by the bedside, would indelibly fix those facts upon the mind.

1. *Food or Diet.*—It has been said that a man must either be a fool or a physician by the time he is forty years old. But as regards food he must either be a fool or a physician long before that age. The young—those under twenty—have to eat to build up tissue, and although it is dangerous for even these to eat to repletion, their digestive organs are strong and healthy, and they can do away with more than grown-up people can. From twenty-five to fifty we ought to eat well and heartily, but as we are no longer growing, it should be remembered that food is now only necessary for the repair of tissue, and in quality and abundance it ought to be in accordance with the waste of our bodies, the amount of labour and fatigue, bodily or mental, we undergo being—aided by appetite—our best guide. After fifty a man is growing old, he cannot take the same amount of exercise, his spirits are not so wildly

exuberant, and his digestion is as a rule weaker; he should therefore be spare in diet, and careful of its quality.

Hurry in eating should be avoided by all; the salivary juices contain a ferment which is absolutely necessary to healthy digestion. Hundreds and thousands who now suffer from dyspepsia, and all its attendant evils and irritabilities, would be thoroughly cured in less than three months, without medicine, did they but adopt the plan of well mingling the food in the mouth before swallowing it.

Fluid is hardly necessary for healthy digestion. Avoid drinking at meals, fluid may be taken *after*. A man who cannot eat his breakfast before drinking his tea ought to make his will, or visit his doctor.

If you cannot have company at dinner, *read*.

Eat only what you know agrees with you, and do not, as a rule, eat between meals.

Never drink anything of a stimulating character on an empty stomach. If you must, through feebleness' sake, have a stimulant, eat a biscuit with it.

Take dinner or supper early in the evening, and if hungry before retiring, a biscuit and a glass of soda-water will induce wholesome, brain-easing slumber. Fruit in the morning is an excellent natural aperient.

2. *Alcohol.*—A cyclist should not require it in any form. If he does not use it he will never miss it, and will be more clear in brain, and lead altogether a more natural life. To those who must and will have stimulants, I say that a modicum of good beer suits an Englishman best—if in health. Draught is better than bottled, and it ought to be taken only towards the end of a meal, and

never in such quantities as to weaken the gastric juices or prevent the stomach from getting a good grasp of the solid food. Port is a dangerous wine to many, so is burgundy. Both tend to make blood too fast, and lead to congestions. It is your blood-filled men who catch colds and inflammations, and succumb the speediest to them. Sauterne is a good summer wine. Clarets I do not think suit our climate. I would rather drink sour buttermilk any day than ordinary claret. Really good malt whiskey diluted with water suits the climate of Scotland. Rum is bad at any price; gin is worse. Champagne, if it be champagne, is wholesome, but should be partaken of in great moderation.

Soda and brandy stimulates, but does not support the system.

3. *Aërated Drinks.*—The Americans murder themselves on these, and Englishmen try to follow their example in summer and whenever they go abroad.

The East Indian thinks a Britisher is bound to be strong because he drinks so much soda-water. He argues thus: The strength that sends a cork flying from a bottle like a shot from a gun, if swallowed, must give force and vim to the frame.

The very reverse is the fact. Mind, I do not say that, taken in moderation, these aërated drinks do harm. Far from it. But it is the constant imbibing of them that does the harm.

Temperance.—The only temperate man, in my estimation, is he who is moderate in everything—in eating, drinking, exercise, and in desires, and thought, and speech.

Temperance of this kind is the key that opens the golden gates of health.

4. *Smoking.*—I have studied the question for years in all its bearings, and have come to the conclusion that a moderate use of *good* tobacco is not injurious to the system. On the contrary, it often does good, if only by allaying fret and worry and banishing weariness, all of which prey upon and weaken the system.

But smoking too much, or smoking your cigars to the bitter end, is most injurious, and smoking very strong tobacco is quite as bad as drinking spirits of wine fresh from the retort.

5. *Tea, Coffee and Cocoa.*—Cocoa is the most nourishing of the three. Get that which is not mixed with starch, and if the digestion be somewhat weak, cocoatina will be best, as it is deprived of most of the oil. Cocoa or coffee is best for breakfast, and either ought to be fully one-half milk.

I am a great advocate for the use of tea. I do not advise men to drink it in the morning, though delicate women may. I hold that, if you have not eaten a too hearty supper, or " looked upon the wine when it was red," that you must have slept well, and therefore do not require a stimulant in the shape of tea. Besides, tea will not induce an appetite. A half-cup of hot water with a few drops of the juice squeezed from a lemon or lime may be taken before breakfast, if appetite be absent, then a turn or two in the open air. If you want to render this hot draught still more tonic and appetising, then, in addition to the squeeze of lemon, add a dessert-spoonful of quassia-water.

Tea, whether cold or hot, is the most harmless and refreshing beverage one can drink on a long journey.

But never drink tea, or coffee either, at a railway-station restaurant; there is no name bad enough for the vile adulterated abomination I have tasted while journeying by rail. I now invariably take my own tea with me in a bottle.

I often travel from the south of England to the extreme north of Scotland, and I have tried both stimulants and tea. When I have drank beer, it invariably made me after a time cold and thirsty, and I had to take more. Arrived at my journey's end, I felt heavy and tired. But now, on tea alone, I can travel the kingdom through, and feel quite able, on alighting at the extreme end of it, to make a pun or crack a joke.

It is Indian tea I use, and I favour Darjeeling, Kangra Valley or Assam. I never drink China tea if I can avoid it, for the same reason that I do not eat French eggs in autumn. China tea, like French eggs, is collected in small quantities, and I happen to know that the collectors of this tea, in travelling over the country, often make use of a sack of it instead of a mattress to sleep on. Fancy that! and Chinamen are not over cleanly. China tea, moreover, is greatly adulterated; Indian is not. From a book on "Tea" which I wrote two or three years ago I cull the following extracts on the making of good tea:

> The *tea-kettle* should be kept scrupulously clean, both inside and out. We cannot expect to make good tea from water boiled in a kettle that is barked inside with lime and other deposits and outside with soot.
>
> The *water.*—This should be soft. We are well aware objections may be taken to this statement by some people who tell us

TEA-MAKING.

that the water should be a happy medium—'twixt the soft and the hard—that hard water prevents the extraction in sufficient quantity of the soluble principle of the tea, while soft water favours the extraction of too much tannin. Well, if they will tell us how to make this happy medium, or where to get it, we would be glad to try it. Meanwhile, we prefer soft water, and will take good care, by not stewing our tea or drawing it too long, to obtain the correct quota of extractive matter and no more. There is nothing to beat rain-water that has been kept underground in large tanks.

The water should be filtered.

The fire over which the kettle boils ought to be as free from smoke as possible, otherwise the water may partake of the flavour of peat, wood, or burning coals, and the tea be spoiled.

Before the water has come to the boil, the teapot should be well warmed and the tea put in. It may then stand for a short time on the hob till the water quite boils—then

The tea should at once be made. We heat the teapot in order to conserve all the caloric in the boiling water. We make the tea as soon as the water comes to the boil, because good tea can be made only with *freshly* boiling water, not boiling water that has been boiled before, or has been kept boiling to long.

Boiled water is flat because it is non-aërated, that is the "why and the wherefore."

Carbonate ot soda should *never* be put in the teapot. It is best, we think, to pour on all the water that is wanted—for the first cups at all events—at once, and not merely "to wet the tea," as it is popularly called.

It is a mistake to add fresh tea to that which has already been made. If more tea or stronger tea is wanted, it ought to be made in another teapot, and a spare one thus often comes in handy.

The best kind of teapot is the old-fashioned brown earthenware one. And what is called a "*cosy*" is hardly ever required, except, perhaps, in winter, but there is always the danger of the tea being left to stew too long under it.

How long, then, should tea draw? From three minutes to seven, according to the kind of tea and character of the water.

Invalids, and people with delicate stomachs (and everybody

else) ought to be most careful to procure tea of superior excellence, and quite free from facing and adulteration, and ought to attend rigidly to the plan of making a cup of good tea, which we have just endeavoured to explain. The invalid should never on any account drink green or scented teas, and the tea that he is to drink, after having been infused for the proper time, say about five minutes, should be poured off the leaves into a well-heated, clean teapot, and served in that, covered by the cosy, if there be one about.

Sugar, milk or cream are mere accessories, but very pleasant ones to the taste of most people. Did ever you try, as a cycling drink, cold tea, without sugar or cream, and a dash of lemon juice in it ?

CHAPTER IX.

ON EXERCISE.—WINTER RIDING.—PURE AIR.—COMMON SENSE ABOUT SLEEP. — THE BATH. — MOUNTAIN DEW *versus* WHISKEY.

*E*XERCISE.—The value of properly and judiciously conducted exercise in the open air cannot well be over-estimated. It is to this fact alone that so many people, young, middle-aged, and even old, who have adopted cycling as a pastime, owe their complete restoration to health and their hopes of a comfortable and happy longevity.

Now, exercise, to be of any use at all, should be taken in moderation, with regularity, and in the open air. Exercise should also be of a kind to give pleasure and to engross all thoughts for the time being, to the entire exclusion of care and worry of all kinds.

With regard to its regularity, let me suppose that you are taking a course of exercise for the purpose of raising your health standard. I may say you are then in the position of a handcart that is being pushed up a hill; a regular, steady, constant force is needed to get the cart to the top of the eminence. What would you think of a man, then, who would give the cart one or two good pushes now and then and abandon it in the intervals? Would the cart not roll back to its first position? Would the man ever succeed in getting it up the hill? No. It is precisely the same with exercise taken intermittently. If you do not go steadily on with it you will never in this world get to the top of the hill of health.

I have often said—and it cannot be *too* often repeated—that of all kinds of exercise the best is cycling, when adopted with wisdom. The only drawback to it is that the propelling force required is different on different parts of the road. Cycling would be a perfect exercise were we to chance on some invention which would make hills easier for us and save our hearts and lungs. Until this is found out, it is for you and for me, reader, to avoid " spurts " as we value our lives. There is seldom such hurry needed on a journey as to prevent us from getting down and walking when we come to a hill which might distress us to ride up. Let your own feelings be your guide; it is my duty as a medical man to tell you that wherever —whether owing to the muddy or hilly condition of the road—riding is unaccompanied with pleasure, your health, not to say your life itself, is in danger.

It is possible I may be considered enthusiastic on the subject of cycling, but I would have all other forms of exercise merely accessory to and leading up to life upon wheels. Take carriage exercise if you like. A ride in a tall dogcart, behind a horse that can go, and through an interesting country, is very exhilarating, and stirs the blood well. Dumb-bells, if taken for half-an-hour every day, and in a scientific and systematic way, so as to bring, group by group, all the muscles of the body into play, is one of the best forms of exercise we possess.

Walking is good, but apt to be monotonous. Lonely walks are objectionable from a health point of view.

Games such as lawn-tennis and cricket are next to cycling in the good they accomplish to both mind and body.

But the whole secret of successful exercise lies in a nut-shell: it must be engrossing, pleasurable, and taken in the open air.

Winter Riding.—Many cyclists, after riding hard all the season, put away the iron horse in November, and do not take it out again till daisy days. This is a great mistake. I approve of winter riding whenever the weather is at all open. If, however, circumstances compel you to put away the cycle, then, as you value your health, substitute some other form of exercise, else—the cart will roll down the hill again.

Pure Air.—This is essential to our well-being. One cannot be too much out of doors, and the rooms we live in should be in winter most thoroughly well ventilated, and not too warm.

It is to me a marvel how editors, clerks and writers can exist in the over-heated stuffy dens they call their "rooms in town." Six weeks of such a life would kill me. But then, to be sure, I am a country bird, and was reared in forests and wilds.

The bedroom should be well aired, but how seldom it is. Talking about the bedroom leads me to say a word or two about

Sleep.—I need not waste space in trying to explain the physiology of sleep. We all know we want it, though we do not always obtain it. But this as often as not is our own fault.

On the other hand, many of us get and take more than we really require.

Let me give a few hints to those who find it difficult to obtain good rest at night, for remember, a dreamful slumber often does more harm than good. I have known people so far gone, that the only exercise they ever got was tossing from side to side in bed during their imperfect and fitful slumbers. This is a deplorable state to be in.

But, mark my words, if you do not obtain good solid rest at night, your health sadly wants seeing to. You may, or you may not, consult a medical man. At all events, you had better ask yourself the following questions, for on the life you lead by day, greatly depends the rest and sleep you obtain at night?

Do I eat and drink judiciously? Do I eat and drink too much? Do I eat between meals, or swamp my stomach with fluid, and thus weaken the gastric juices?

Do I work too hard, and too late in the evening, thus over-gorging the capillaries of my brain and weakening their resiliency? Do I think too hard and worry too much? Is life to me all a fever? All a game in which I am staking my health against the chances of winning fame or money that I cannot hope to live to enjoy?

Do I take exercise enough to make me feel pleasantly tired?

Do I live enough in the fresh air?

Do I get my skin to act well enough by means of the bracing morning tub, and an occasional Turkish bath?

SLEEP.

Have I ever tried to live for a time by rule and systematically?

Is my bedroom sufficiently ventilated? Is it too hot? Do I have too many bedclothes, well-knowing that these ought to be light, and only moderately warm? Do I sleep on a feather bed, when a mattress would be far better? Do I burn a light in my room, and scare the goddess of sleep away?

Do I smoke too much?

Do I use narcotics, knowing that their constant use leads to that most terrible of all deaths — a nervous, frightened, trembling death? (The lower animals never fear the approach of death, although I am convinced they often know it is coming. And death to human beings should be like falling asleep.)

Now, the answers to the above questions are all evident enough, only they are worthy of the greatest consideration.

I may add, however, that in cases where the mind is far too active to admit of sleep, and the person keeps tumbling about and thinking about different subjects every minute, it is far better to light the candle and read. This at least will steady the thoughts and gradually weary the over-excited brain.

I have now to say a very few words about the *bath*, because I believe that bathing ought to go hand-in-hand with cycling.

It would serve no useful purpose to give here any lengthened account of the skin and its uses in the animal economy. Everyone knows, or ought to know, that if it be not in good working order, the health cannot be up to the mark.

A person with a badly acting skin may exist, but he cannot be said to live. Some people merely take a warm bath of a Saturday night. This is what a Scotchman would call " ill-less, goodless."

The best way of securing free action of the skin, well-braced nerves, and an almost perfect immunity from colds and coughs all the year round, is to wash the body all over every morning with warm or hot water, and a mild transparent soap, then immediately after well laving the head and brow with cold water, to plunge into the tub and sponge all over twice or thrice with cold water.

Ladies and delicate people may have the chill off, but it does not do half the good.

Those who can stand it should have the cold shower-bath.

There should be two handfuls of sea-salt mixed in every bucket of water.

Then immediately rub well dry with rough towels, dress quickly, and walk ten minutes in the open air before breakfast, or take a turn of the dumb-bells out of doors.

A Turkish or hot-air bath should be taken at least once a fortnight.

Some people suffer from dullness or lowness of spirits at times without any known cause. In such a case be sure there is something coursing in your veins, bile or acid, perhaps, that needs elimination, and the hot-air bath will do it.

Messrs. Allen, of Marylebone Lane, Oxford Street, make the portable Turkish bath. It is beyond all praise, and has saved many a valuable life.

THE BATH.

Remember these facts about the hot-air bath: 1. It is better to be taken in the recumbent position—in a bed, for example; but this bed should be well aired afterwards, or mischief may occur. 2. Ten minutes to a quarter of an hour is long enough to remain after sweating has fairly commenced. 3. If, as a cure for biliousness, low spirits, or rheumatic gout, you commence with hot-air baths, you must persist for some time, even if they at first seem to disagree.

There is probably no time a person enjoys a bath more than after a good long run, providing there be time to take it, before dinner.

For example, you come in heated and pleasantly tired, and find there is three-quarters of an hour to spare. Well, retire to the dressing-room. Rest for a few minutes, then leisurely undress. Lather down now with warm water and soap, then have your sponge bath, and dress again quietly, in well-aired clothing.

Meanwhile, in your own spirits-of-wine conjurer, the water is boiling for a cup of Darjeeling. How refreshing! You will have an appetite for dinner, nor will it be an artificial one such as some men invoke by the aid of spirits.

By the way, I am sometimes asked what is the best kind of spirits to use, if it be deemed necessary. My reply is Scotch or Irish whiskey, but it *must* be old and it *must* be malted. In riding through a district in Scotland last summer, I passed a large distillery, and was astonished and shocked to be told by the clergyman of the parish that it was nearly all made from maize, and on the raw-grain and sulphuric acid principle.

" Stands Scotland where it did ? " asked Burns.

No, my dear departed shade, in does not—in the matter of whiskey. The romance is evaporated from the mountain dew. It is only fair to add, however, that most Scotch wine merchants do keep good malt whiskey if people ask for it and are willing to pay a fair price.

But new or raw-grain whiskey is simply poison, and the Legislature should prevent its being sold, unless duly labelled as such.

CHAPTER X.

Facts about Physic.

MOST of the contents of this chapter are extracted from my "Companion to the Gordon Pocket Medicine Chest," a little book which, though its author, I may be permitted to say contains many truths in a minimum of space. It would indeed be well if all in search of health would read them and lay them to heart. Well, when in the hey-day of health they may not care to do so, only a time may come when they will be found useful, and mayhap a boon.

On Drugs in General.

The number of drugs used nowadays by professional men in good practice is comparatively small; physicians are careful, however, to have these of well-proved efficacy and neatly compounded. The notion so long held by the public, that a drug must be nauseous and difficult to take to be effectual, has now entirely exploded, and a doctor will much rather prescribe his remedies in a handy and elegant form than in the old-fashioned and cumbrous method. Speaking from experience, it is quite a boon to a medical man to find on a chemist's counter the exact medicine he was about to order, ready compounded, and that too by firms who study to present him with the best formulæ and most useful remedies in the neatest and most elegant guise. It is a boon to the medical man, and it is also a boon to his patients.

The Value of Medicine.

The indiscriminate use of medicine, and too much self-doctoring, are greatly to be deprecated. One of the ablest physicians that ever lived said, on retiring into private life, "I am tired of guessing."

If even medical men, who spend their whole lives in the study of disease, are often doubtful of the correctness of their diagnosis, and hesitate before administering a drug, how much more careful ought he to be to whom the science of medicine is a sealed book? But, nevertheless, skilled advice is not always at hand when required, and in these days of higher education and advanced knowledge of all subjects, it is the duty of everyone to make himself acquainted with a few facts about Materia Medica and minor surgery. Help given at the moment it is wanted is often instrumental in saving life, when delay might mean death.

The plan of taking a supply of really good reliable medicines on a tour, either by land or sea, is greatly to be commended. A guide to their use should also be carried, but, nevertheless, these are only intended for use in emergencies, while a physician or surgeon is being summoned, or for slight ailments. It displaces the use of secret nostrums, which often lead to serious complications when used indiscriminately.

Facts about Physic.

Drugs are divided by practitioners into certain classes, the medicines in each having various virtues in common. Let us say a word or two about the more useful of these:—

1. *Antacids.*—A much abused class of medicines. They are used to correct acidity either of the blood, the urine, or system at large. They are, however, most commonly used by people to remove acidity of the stomach; but what should not be forgotten about them is this—they are merely palliative, their action is only temporary, and if persisted in they are very likely to make matters worse instead of better. Acidity of the stomach is a symptom that calls aloud for attention to the general health and a proper *régime*. The commonest and safest antacids are the bi-carbonates of soda and potash, and are most convenient in the form of compressed tablets. The compressed tablets of soda mint will be found in the Gordon Medicine Chest.

2. *Antispasmodics.*—Medicines used to remove spasm or pain. Remember this about them—the cause of the pain or spasm must be sought for and removed before much benefit is to be expected from the drug itself. An emetic may be needed or an aperient. Brandy in small doses is often invaluable, so is chlorodyne, but these should be followed at a suitable interval by an aperient, and

FACTS ABOUT PHYSIC. 79

in all cases rest should be enjoined. We may say here that rest and warmth in bed enable nature alone to get over any complaint that is not of a deadly character.

3. *Astringents.*—These are used most commonly for the cure of diarrhœa, and externally for the healing of cuts, bruises, or sores of any kind. As diarrhœa is generally an effort of nature to get rid of some offending matter, the complaint should not be suddenly checked, but a little port wine and brandy may be taken, well diluted, lest it cause acidity; after this a dose of chlorodyne will do good. The food should be light, and no meat partaken of till the trouble has entirely gone. The best internal or external astringent for the tourist is Hazeline.

4. *Aperients.*—These form a class of very much abused medicines. Without doubt, the body cannot long be maintained in health if the system be bound up and dry, but it should be kept open if possible by natural means—exercise, the morning bath, and a judicious amount of fruit and vegetables. But when opening medicine becomes a necessity, what is wanted is a gentle aperient, one that will not only increase the flow of the secretions, but also the natural movements of the alimentary canal. A very good aperient pill is called the Vegetable Laxative, and will, we doubt not, be found very efficacious, and it is also safe. An aperient may be followed next morning by a white draught, such as a glass of Pullna or Friedrichshall water, or the good old-fashioned Seidlitz powder. We much prefer to recommend the natural waters, and we think that country druggists would be consulting their own interests by selling these by the glass, instead of only by the bottle, as they now do.

5. *Diaphoretics.*—Medicines to induce perspiration. A good sweat is often invaluable in curing an incipient cold, or in cutting short an attack of rheumatism, and many other painful ailments. Again, we say, get this sweat by natural means, if possible; but we may assist nature. The Turkish bath is the best means to this end. Messrs. Allen and Son, 21, Marylebone Lane, Oxford Street, make a portable Turkish bath, and the whole subject of bathing is fully discussed in the little shilling manual sold by this firm. Another plan by which a free perspiration may be induced is the old-fashioned one of taking a hot drink, bathing the feet and legs in hot water with a handful of mustard in it, and going

to bed, with an extra covering; but in addition to this, a dose of compound ipecac. powder should be taken. It has been put it this chest,

6. *Diuretics.*—Medicines which increase the flow of the urine. As a rule they should only be prescribed by a medical man, but when the skin is over-active and the body very hot, as on summer days after exercise, a teaspoonful of the sweet spirits of nitre is very cooling and effective. It is also very safe.

7. *Expectorants.*—On the advent of a cold accompanied by a cough, it is always judicious to consult a doctor. Two very safe and effective remedies for ordinary coughs are Pill Squill Co. and Hazeline. They contain no opium, which is a drug that only a medical man can prescribe with safety, yet nearly all the cough mixtures of the shops contain opium in some form or another. Digestives: It is but right here to say a word for some new preparations now or recently introduced by Messrs. Burroughs and Wellcome, especially the Kepler Extract of Malt, their Peptonic Tablets—a supply of which will be found in the case—and their Extractum Pancreatis. What we consider these most valuable for is their tonic and dissolvent qualities, by which the partaker is enabled to digest and assimilate a much larger proportion of nutriment than he could otherwise do. They are thus tonics in the truest sense of the word, but they are more, for they so strengthen the body and the lungs as to obviate the tendency to take colds. They thus prevent all forms of lung mischief. Pancreatic extract, or the extract of malt, or the Kepler solution of cod liver oil with extract of malt, can also be taken instead of cod liver oil, in cases where that medicine disagrees, or the oil and extracts can be taken at the same time. We constantly prescribe them in every stage of lung mischief, and always in general debility, however induced.

8. *Tonics.*—People as a rule take these too often. We have this to say about them, that they should not be taken longer than three weeks at a time; that they are best taken only twice a day, and that during the course the system should be kept free by taking an aperient about once a week. The vegetable tonic will be found a most useful one, as it purifies the blood and strengthens both nerves and muscles. Peptonic (digestive) Tablets may be taken at the same time, or the Kepler Extract of Malt or pan-

FACTS ABOUT PHYSIC.

creatic extract. We have a special remedy for cases of chronic rheumatism, but it must not be forgotten that, in nine cases out of ten, the cause of rheumatism is to be found in bad digestion and a badly-acting skin.

HINTS ABOUT PRESCRIBING

A weakly person, an old person, or a delicate lady may take these medicines with the utmost confidence; they are also easily swallowed. In prescribing medicines generally, the following hints should be borne in mind :—

1. Do not give medicine without occasion.
2. Never give a dangerous remedy.
3. Buy medicines from respectable chemists; you will in this way be sure to get them pure and free from adulteration.
4. Do not give aperients if the system be open; nor tonics if nerves and muscles be strong; nor sweating powders if the patient has soon to be exposed to the weather; nor narcotics if they can possibly be done without.
5. Do not give medicine of any kind without at the same time regulating the diet. If medicines are to be given, the sooner the better; a stitch in time saves nine stitches, in the side or anywhere else.
6. Only a medical man should prescribe for a child

CHAPTER XI.

ADVICE TO LADIES.—WEAKLY PEOPLE AND INVALIDS.—AILMENTS FOR WHICH CYCLING IS RECOMMENDED.

I DO not deny that many ladies are as strong and hardy in constitution as most men folks, and, therefore, I ought probably to apologise for classing them with invalids. But the rule is that men can do more and stand more on the cycle or off it than ladies can.

Among weakly people I count the very young, say those under sixteen, the aged, and those who have feeble constitutions, while the class of invalids I address is that only which suffers from complaints in which cycling is not counter-indicated.

I will now, for hypothesis sake, take the case of a not over-robust person of either sex, who, on reading this book of mine, or my "Health Upon Wheels," feels a dawning hope that cycling may—as it does in thousands of cases—set him or her on a healthful footing. That all fits of dyspepsia and despondency will soon be forgotten under the new *régime*, and appetite will be no longer capricious, nor irritability of temper and peevishness a common complaint.

Would I advise such an individual to at once buy a tricycle and commence riding? Certainly not. I would have him go first to a medical man, and state his case and make known his hopes and wishes. If he says that

WEAKLY PEOPLE.

the exercise, not carried to excess, will, in all probability, do good, then all right. If he says that to ride would be dangerous, then seek for better health by taking some other form of gentle open-air exercise.

Now, I will suppose it is spring time, and that the long delightful days of summer are all before you. Do not be in a great hurry to purchase the cycle, for I seriously advise you to go under a kind of mild preliminary training. Your muscles are not now in form, and if they be not, depend upon it that the heart is also flabby. But judicious exercise will strengthen every organ of the body.

Let this exercise be walking. Determine to live by rule for six weeks before you commence practising on the tricycle. Live fairly well, rise betimes and take the bracing bath I have already recommended *every morning*, however cold the weather may be.

And however cold, or even *wet*, the weather is, you must take your daily walk. For the first week three miles a day will be enough, at the same hour daily; the second week let it be four, then five, then six.

Do not walk briskly the first week, and if at all fatigued, rest a few minutes anywhere out of doors, then go on again. It is truly wonderful the amount of benefit that accrues from this simple plan.

Shall you take tonics? Well, towards the end of your walking course you may. Iron and quinine in small doses suits most people. Or pills of the phosphate of iron, or if the liver be at fault, small doses of the dilute nitro-hydrochloric acid in the infusion of chiretta or quassia.

But I wish it to be borne in mind, that far more good will accrue from constant exercise, the bath and regularity of living than from any medicine one can take.

Cod liver oil with the Kepler Extract of Malt deserves special mention here. But, then, this is not really a medicine, but a food. Cod liver oil is the most easily digested of all fats, and is at the same time the most nourishing.

Well, I must now imagine you are tolerably fit for exercise on wheels. It will be time now to look out for a cycle. If a lady, it is my opinion you cannot beat the " Salvo ;" if a gentleman, you will find the handsome " Ranelagh" one of the easiest-going and prettiest machines in the market.

At all events, get a good new machine, not a heavy one. Learn all about its mechanism and the way it should be kept and oiled before you attempt to ride.

You will soon learn to ride fairly well, but months will pass before you can rush along with the least possible expenditure of power. The most difficult thing to get up to is the treadling. You must not push a rising treadle, it must have fairly turned the corner before power is applied.

Try, especially if a lady, to sit erect and gracefully on the seat or saddle. Nothing looks worse than to see an individual swaying about on his cycle like a scarecrow on a windy day.

Learn to ride on level road, and do not be disappointed if it comes hard on you at first. This is sure to be the case for two reasons. (1) You have not yet mastered the stroke; (2) your muscles are still soft, and nervous system not in order ; but nerves and muscles both soon get " hard " with constant cycling exercise in the open air.

When you do commence to do a little touring, be careful not to make the journeys too long at first. You may do yourself serious injury by even one day's over-fatigue. Imitate the swallows—don't make long flights at first. Vary your routes as much as possible, for health is to be gained on the cycle as much from change of scene and recreation as from actual exercise. It is the beauty of cycling that muscle is made and mind is exhilarated at one and the same time.

Dress for the Road.—After all said and done, we are much in the same position as we were a dozen years ago in the matter of dress, except that Dr. Jaeger has brought forward his all-woollen garments.

The sum and substance of the subject is this: We should dress for comfort, and, to some extent, for appearance. Ladies, at all events, should look neat while riding, and neither ladies nor gentlemen should have trailing garments or anything loose that would be likely to catch among the works and cause an accident.

The clothes worn should be warm and light, and a change of underclothing should invariably be carried in the cycling basket.

I do not approve of tricyclists using the knapsack; it is not good for the chest.

I do not like the uniform usually worn by clubs. It is too close in front. The chest ought to have full freedom. Indeed, a thoroughly comfortable club uniform "built" on scientific principles has yet to be invented.

I may add that heavy wraps for the neck should be abjured. The idea of boas for ladies is too ridiculous. A light silken muffler is best, and the neck should never be kept too warm when riding.

For contents of cycling basket, for comfort on the road, and a variety of other useful hints, I must refer the reader to my other book called "Health upon Wheels."* It is but fair to myself to say that the copyright belongs entirely to the publishers, and that I have no other object in recommending it except that of benefiting my fellow-cyclists.

Cycling tourists, especially ladies and weakly people, ought to take the greatest care of the feet, never allowing them to remain any length of time damp.

Cold Feet.—This is a complaint that a great many people, more especially ladies, suffer from. It ought not to be forgotten that it is generally a symptom of unequal circulation, and points to a somewhat weakened or congenitally weak heart. Now, cycling will either mend matters or make matters much worse. This may seem a solecism, but it is true, for judicious cycling strengthens every muscle in the body, and the heart as well, of course, but fatiguing cycling, and spurting, actually stretches and weakens the muscular tissue of the heart, and therefore it is less able to propel the warm blood to the extremities.

Treatment.—You must attend to the rules of health, and obey the laws of hygiene to the letter. Take exercise in abundance in the open air, but never over-fatigue yourself. Wash the feet in *cold* water before going to bed. Do not have a hot water-bottle, as some recommend, but ladies may wear bed-socks.

The medicines that do most good are Parish's Chemi-

---

* Published by Iliffe and Son, 98 Fleet Street, E.C. Price 1 2 post free.

cal Food, cod liver oil, cod liver oil with Kepler's Extract of Malt, hypophosphite of lime, one grain to two grains in a little water twice a day, or the following prescription, which is a most excellent tonic in a variety of forms of debility :—

℞

  Extr. Nucis Vomicæ ... grs. xii.
  Zinci. Sulph. ... ... ,, xxx.
  Extr. Rhei. ... ... ʒi ♏.

Ft. pil. xxiv. Label: One twice a day for an adult.

Attention should be paid to the teeth if you wish to be well. The toothbrush should be used after every meal, not merely in the morning. Use a softish brush and a powder that does not contain anything likely to scour or wear the enamel.

When upon extended tours, beware of damp beds. The best plan is always to imagine they are damp, and spread a shawl over the sheet.

Drinks on the Road.—This is a much-debated subject. The best plan is to ride so easily that you do not need any drinks. Milk and soda is often useful, but apt to disagree with delicate stomachs. Buttermilk, when it can be had, is better; cold, weak tea is best of all. Never drink beer or spirits when touring; cold spring water is much to be preferred.

Who should Ride? — Almost everyone. Exceptions: The very young and the very weakly, or those suffering from disease of any important internal organ. I am glad to have this opportunity of lifting up my voice against the riding of cycles by children. If you want a boy or girl to grow up ill-formed and awkward, and all out of joint, make him or her the present of a tricycle.

A Few Ailments for which Cycling is Recommendable :—
General debility without actual disease.
Chronic rheumatism.
Anæmia, or poverty of blood.
Predisposition to colds.
Constipation.
Corpulency.
Dyspepsia.
Eruptions (such as pimples or acne).
Giddiness.
Biliousness.
Gout (tendency to).
Gravel (tendency to).
Headaches.
Acidity of system (stomach and blood).
Joints (various chronic affections of).
Liver (various chronic ailments of).
Loss of appetite, &c.
Low spirits, or *ennui*.
Lumbago (the tendency to).
Neuralgia.
Nervousness (in all its branches).
Old age (premature).
Piles (tendency to).
Sleeplessness.
Stones in ducts, &c. (tendency to).
Diarrhœa (only the tendency to).
Wasting palsy.
Water brash.
Writer's cramp (conjoined with other remedies).

Invalids and delicate people who have the intention of taking an extended tour or a cycling holiday should put in their basket or portmanteau a few medicines likely to be useful on an emergency. The "Gordon" Pocket Medicine Chest contains everything that can be needed.

Now, my advice to those who have made up their minds to become cycling tourists is to take the train to the town or village they mean to make their headquarters, and this should be as far away from their own homes as possible. If you can leave every care behind, and all business, a cycling holiday in a suitable district will do more for you in a month than medicine could in ten years.

A Word to Parents.—Cycling is the worst form of exercise for a delicate child. Indeed, I never feel happy when I see any girl or boy under the age of fifteen on a cycle. *Verbum sap.*

SIMPLE AILMENTS AND THEIR SAFE TREATMENT.

For bruises, burns, wounds, abrasions, and for varicose inflammations and sores, Hazeline may be used undiluted by means of bandages or Lawton's absorbent cotton.

For soreness, lameness, and for chapped, chafed, or irritated surfaces, as prickly heat, etc., apply undiluted, especially after bathing.

For hæmorrhoids, the best method is to administer from ten to thirty drops daily, and at the same time employ it as an injection, clear, or diluted with an equal bulk of water, or it may be applied frequently as a lotion by means of Lawton's cotton.

In hæmorrhages (especially passive), and in diarrhœa, dysentery, and inflammation of the bowels, from ten drops to half a teaspoonful may be taken frequently till relieved.

In inflammation of the lungs, pleurisy, asthma, bronchitis, and sore throat, it is best used as a spray or with an atomizer, also applying it externally.

F

In ozœna and ordinary catarrh it may be snuffled up the nostrils, diluted with an equal bulk of warm water, or applied by means of a camel's-hair pencil or a spray.

In purulent ophthalmia and inflammation of the eyes, it may be diluted with an equal bulk of warm water, and applied by means of Lawton's absorbent cotton.

For ulcerated sore mouth, tender gums, toothache, and bleeding sockets, Hazeline may be employed as a mouth wash.

NOTE.—Hazeline is decomposed by contact with metals or mineral salts.

BLEEDING (called also Hæmorrhage).—Keep cool. Notice the colour of the blood: if arterial, it is bright red and spurts out; if venous, it is darker. From a vein it is called passive hæmorrhage; from an artery, active. Pressure and Hazeline will always arrest passive hæmorrhage. To stem the flow: 1. Raise the bleeding part higher than rest of the body. Do not give brandy, even if faint. 2. Apply pressure, if an artery is bleeding, between the wound and the heart; pressure applied by finger, or bandages or pads, or both. 3. Apply cold to bleeding part; styptics, of which Hazeline is the best.

BLEEDING FROM NOSE.—Keep upright. Apply Hazeline; also snuff, or inject it up the nostrils, and put cold key or ice on the spine. Cold applications. Apply cold to the nape of the neck.

WOUNDS OF THE HEAD.—Cuts or wounds of the head bleed very freely, owing to the vascularity of the scalp. Do not be alarmed even if the head be covered with blood; wash thoroughly with cold water and look for the wound, which may be very small, and yet bleed enormously. Pour Hazeline or Eucalyptine into the cut (if a large one, bring the edges together), and apply firm pressure by means of a piece of cork or wood wrapped in rag. Until that can be obtained, press the wound firmly against the skull with the fingers. Fracture of the skull rarely occurs, and is recognised by feeling inside the cut. In all cases of arterial bleeding, where bright red blood pumps out, send for a doctor; until he arrives act as instructed.

WOUNDS OR CUTS ON THE HAND. ARTERIAL BLEEDING.—The bleeding may be arrested by holding a cork firmly in the palm of the hand, and if necessary putting a bandage round the wrist with a hard substance pressing on the pulse

SIMPLE AILMENTS. 91

BLEEDING FROM THE FORE-ARM.—Roll up a handkerchief into a ball, place it in the bend of the elbow, and flex the fore-arm firmly so as to retain it there.

WOUNDS TO THE UPPER ARM.—Roll up a towel or napkin, place it in the arm-pit, and press the arm firmly to the side. The same rules apply to the feet and legs. The pad to be placed behind the knee or in the groin as required, and the limb flexed.

BROKEN BONES.—Fracture of any kind is a serious accident. Place the sufferer in an easy position, till assistance arrives Carry carefully to nearest house. Give brandy if no bleeding. Send for nearest surgeon.

BONES OUT OF PLACE.—If a joint be dislocated, it is immovably fixed in altered position. Keep the sufferer at rest, and send for nearest surgeon. Attempts at reduction may be tried at once, by making extension, and guiding the dislocated bone to its original position. Apply Hazeline at once to reduce swelling and alleviate the pain.

BRAIN, SHOCK TO.—This may be caused by a fall. It is usually called a "stun." It may or may not be serious. Consult a doctor. Put patient to bed. Give no brandy or other stimulants.

BRUISES AND CONTUSIONS.—Hazeline should be applied to prevent swelling and discolouration. Nothing else except that and rest will do any good. If a joint is bruised, gentle and long-continued friction—after the pain is gone—will reduce the swelling. Before the pain is gone, a warm poultice should be used, medicated with laudanum.

BURNS.—If the skin be broken by burn or scald, better consult a physician. In meantime apply Hazeline or bicarbonate of soda. If not broken, the application of spirits of turpentine for two or three minutes will entirely remove the pain. If any shock, give brandy and sal volatile.

FAINTING AND FITS.—Carry person to fresh air, lay down with limbs straight out, and head, neck, and shoulders on a level with body, or *slightly* raised. Remove collar, etc., rub the hands, apply ammonia to nostrils, and dash or sprinkle a little cold water on chest and face. Apply cold to back of chest. Give a little brandy when sufficiently recovered, but not much.

SHOCK.—Put patient in warm bed. Put hot water to feet and pit of stomach, and give occasionally a little brandy and water.

SPRAINS.—Hazeline, Eucalyptine, or other soothing applications. *Rest* and leeches, if much pain and swelling.

CHAPTER XII.*

"Do" or "Dont," or Suicide Made Easy.

ALTHOUGH cycling, when judiciously managed, when wisdom sits upon the saddle and prudence guides the helm, is an exercise of so charming and wholesome a nature, that the goddess Hygeia herself might be represented riding on three wheels, and crowned with laurel leaves, still the sport, as our young "bloods" love to call it, if carried to excess, or recklessly and thoughtlessly engaged in, may, and often does, induce a state of body, and I may as well add mind, that is very much the reverse of healthy.

I am somewhat ashamed of the length of that last sentence. Well, let it stand, and if I cannot be laconic I will try at least to be truthful.

There are a great many cyclists in this favoured land of ours—and I suppose such persons are not wanting in America either—who seem bent on committing suicide by running themselves to death.

It is always a pity to spoil a good intention, and if there be any truth in the doctrine of natural selection and survival of the fittest, the world would really be better without these would-be suicides. It is, therefore, with a view to help such people to a better state of being that

---

*N.B.—This chapter is "wrote kinder sarkastic."

this chapter is written, and the following hints are given :—

1.—In your choice of a cycle do not be guided by the advice of your friends, however large their experience may be, or however scientific their ideas. Suit yourself. Get the biggest wheeled, dashiest-looking machine you can find in the market. Have the wheels very high, especially if you are not very tall yourself. When the toes barely touch the treadles, although you have not the power over your machine you would otherwise possess, still appearance is everything, and it is nice to be looked at and admired.

Besides, I know no better plan of inducing that most elegant of all deformities of the feet, called by the surgical profession *talipes equinus*,* or horse-foot, than riding a cycle a mile too tall for you.

N.B.—A mitigated form of this species of club-foot is rather an advantage to a lady than otherwise, for do not most of our fashionable fair sex aim at such a malformation, else why those high-heeled boots?

2.—Get the heaviest machine in the market. A large, heavy machine infers strength in the rider. No matter how weakly he may appear, people will be sure to say he has the "go" in him, and that he is wiry if not very muscular.

3.—A moderate degree of wholesome cycling increases

---

* "*Talipes equinus* is characterised by elevation or the heel and tension of the tendon Achilles. In slight cases the heel may merely be raised a few lines above the ground, and it will be found on examination that it cannot be bent forwards to an acute angle with the leg. In severe cases the foot may be extended in nearly a straight line with the leg, and the patient walks on his toes, which are placed at a right angle to the foot."—Erichson's Surgery, Vol. II., page 308.

the size of the calves of the legs. Injudicious riding deteriorates them. What of that, if you do not happen to possess calves like a Scottish Highlander, buy a pair of pads. They are to be had, I am told, and although there cannot be much strength in them, nevertheless they will do for make-believes.

4.—Be sure to join a club, especially if you have a neat figure. Artemus Ward said once that his main object in giving lectures was to show off his clothes (evening dress). Let this be your principal reason for joining a club.

5.—When riding in club dress never unbutton your coat, it looks untidy, and tidiness is before comfort any day. Wear plenty of watch-chain over your uniform—this also looks nice, and causes servant-maids to stare at you and after you. Give yourself all the airs you can, especially at hotel bars; chaff the landlady, and call the barmaid "Sally."

6.—Wear your uniform on every possible occasion, wet day or dry day, in sunshine or rain. When your club dress is plentifully bespattered in mud you look double the individual, twice the hero, in Sally's eyes.

7.—When riding with your club keep well up with them. Never mind how young you are—keep up. Never mind how thin you are—keep up. Should your ribs be as protrusive as that of an old blood mare's on her way to the knacker's—keep up. Never mind how you gasp and pant and perspire—keep up. Cramps may follow such reckless riding, and restless nights as well—never mind, keep up.

8.—When riding alone imagine you are in training, try

SUICIDE MADE EASY.

to beat all known 'gainst-time-records; spurt like fury. Don't dismount in going uphill. No, rush the hills, and hang the odds.

[N.B.—Attention to rules 7 and 8 hardly ever fail to induce temporary engorgement of the liver, with dyspepsia and, perhaps, a little kidney mischief to follow; spleen and kidneys, too, get gorged with blood, and press on surrounding organs, and on the nerves of organic life, inducing a fine feeling of irritability of temper and system, with more or less of a homicidal tendency, especially on the mornings after. Attention to rules 7 and 8 is sure to lead in the long run to either dilatation or enlargement of the heart, and thus by slow degrees to the grave.]

9.—Smoke by all means. If very young, learn on the sly. Smoke the very cheapest of tobacco. A penny cigar *looks* as well as a fourpenny one.

10.—What shall you drink? Pray don't let that question trouble you. Drink when, where, what, and as much as you choose. Don't have it too weak, anyhow. Never drink butermilk, tea, soda-and-milk, or a lemon squash. If you feel sleepy and not the thing after a glass or two of beer when on the road, have a glass or two more—keep it up.

11.—Let your nights at the club be wet ones. Eat and drink whatever you can get hold of. Talk, sing, laugh, smoke, be generally jolly; keep it up, and don't go home till morning.

12.—Morning headaches are best dispelled by a brandy and soda. If one isn't enough, take another, or a third. What's the odds so long's you're happy.

13.—Never think of having a bath of a morning. Cold bathing tends to strengthen the system and lengthen life. What do you want of long life? Isn't yours the midge's motto, " a short life and a merry ?"

14.—Always eat to repletion, and it is a good plan to mount your cycle and have a ride immediately after breakfast or luncheon.

15.—Another good plan is to take a " peg " or two of brandy neat after a full meal.

16.—Evenings spent in stuffy, grog-steaming, pipe-reeking rooms have an excellent effect in softening the muscular tissue and weakening the nerves.

17.— Should temporary ill-health mar your career, go in for self-doctoring, pour in aperients into your system, and take tonics by the pound or pint. Or, better still, let a chemist prescribe for you, especially a young one ; or, failing this, buy and use patent medicines, those that are warranted to cure two diametrically opposite states of system, such as diarrhœa and constipation, plethora and anæmia, or adiposity and debility, are the best for your purpose.

18.—When damp with perspiration after a long ride, don't change your underclothing, don't have a rub down all over or a bath ; if anyone advises you to do so laugh him to scorn—say " 'My dear sir, I'm not an old wife yet, a damp shirt never hurt me, I've got the constitution of a horse," then go and sit in a draught, and have a draught—beer that is a little hard is as good a thing as any.

19.—Always come straight in from a long ride and sit down to a meal ; the nerves are then in a fine weak condition; the gastric juices at a minimum, and the stomach will have rare fun before it can get rid of the load it is sure to receive.

20.—You cannot eat too quickly. The diastase of the salivary juices are absolutely necessary for the perfect digestion of the food. " Bother the juices," you say, " and bother chemistry and physiology, I'll do as I like and keep it up."

21.—Just before sitting down to dinner, if you find that you have no appetite, have any one, or two if you like, of the following appetisers: gin and bitters, sherry and bitters, brandy with curaçoa, or brandy neat.

22.—Always sleep in a badly-ventilated room, on a feather bed, and with oceans of heavy blankets.

23.—Always ride recklessly, especially going downhill or round corners. A spill or two—if they are good ones—have been known to possess a most material power to hasten the end.

24.—Don't on any account go in for preliminary training and attention to the state of your health, as advised by me at page 83 of this little work. No; begin your spring-riding with a noble disregard for all the golden rules of the Hygeian goddess. So shall you succeed.

I could add much more, but I think that if these twenty-four rules are laid to heart and obeyed to the letter, or even half the letter, the merriest cycling youth will find he will go downhill as fast as he could desire. Even if he should fall short of actual suicide, he will at all events have the satisfaction of knowing that he has made an old man of himself before his time.

CHAPTER XIII.

Hobbies and Health.—Recreation.—On Growing Old.—Pastime Studies for Cyclists.

THOUGH not by nature of a wildly sanguine temperament, still, if I am to judge from the kindly reception many other books of mine have received from my friend The People, I may feel confident that the present little work will be read by thousands of intelligent men and women. It is precisely because my readers are intelligent, that it would ill-become me to write even a brief dissertation on any of the pastime studies which I am going to recommend for cyclists who loiter along the road for health and pleasure sake. My earnest desire is not book-making or copy-building, but the writing of that which shall be found useful.

I have long held the opinion that hobbies have a great effect for good on the health. Indeed, I may put it more strongly and state, without fear of contradiction, that if a man possesses a genuine and wholesome hobby, and throws a good deal of his mind—say soul even—into it, he possesses a prophylactic against fifty per cent. of the ailments that afflict the human race. For the mind and body are so thoroughly one, or—let me put it in different language, lest I be accused of being a materialist—the mind and body are so thoroughly *en rapport*, that not only can the one not be out of joint without the other suffering, but by engaging the mind in some pleasant pursuit you rest, calm and strengthen the body, and *vice versâ*. Hence the benefit of having a hobby.

Are you a brain-worker, closely confined for many hours a day in a probably not over well-ventilated office ? Then recreation and exercise of body after hours will ease the over-tired capillaries, and allow the brain itself to rest and revivify.

Are you working out of doors all day manually? Then study in the evening would be actual rest for you, or pleasurable excitement in the form of amusement. Join a whist or chess club, or, better still, a music club, or, best of all, a histrionic society. Thousands have by nature, gifts that if trained and exercised under proper supervision would lead to success on the stage. But a long and severe training is necessary to the smallest degree of histrionic success.

The following extract is from a paper in Cassell's Magazine, by a Family Doctor, and ought to be read and well considered by everyone. If there be a single line in it which is not worthy of being written, I shall be glad to hear of it through the medium of my publishers :

> Well, now, it seems to me that the true meaning of the word " recreation " is very well given in most of our dictionaries, viz , " relief or refreshment after toil or labour, amusement, diversion."
>
> In order to be truly healthful, in every sense of the word, recreation must be of a kind to entirely relieve both body and mind from their *status quo* during work or toil. All thoughts must be for a time diverted into an entirely new and pleasantly interesting channel, so as to rest most completely that other portion of the brain which presides over the thoughtful performance of the duties of the day. The kind of recreation that is

chosen must therefore depend, in a great measure, upon the sort of labour that has been performed. What is rest to one man would be labour to another.

Recreation ought to be in every way the converse to labour; if it be not so, it is not rest. From this it may be seen that the individual himself must choose that form of recreation which is best suited for his health.

But the busiest men among us, even those to whom work is really pleasure, should remember that recreation or relaxation is in reality a necessary of health and life itself. To use a plain and homely simile : well-timed, well-chosen recreation is to our bodies and minds, or to these hearts of ours which are beating, beating night and day, what oil is to the bearings of an engine, it saves wear and tear, and makes the long rough road of life seem shorter and smoother to us.

Brain-workers probably need daily recreation more than any other class of individuals. It is a pity that it is the custom with so many of them to sacrifice the precious hours of the night to work that might be done far better and more brilliantly in the morning, or in the forenoon. I do not speak unadvisedly, but from long experience, when I say that the hours between the evening meal—whether it be dinner or supper—and bed-time should be devoted entirely to rest from labour, combined with, if possible, recreation. The sleep thereafter would be far more useful and refreshing, and in seven hours after retiring to rest the brain would be ready to commence work again with healthier blood in it, and with clearer and therefore more critical perceptions.

The purer and more wholesome the air in which, be they what they may, our recreations are enjoyed the better. Pure air can usually be secured at home in winter and spring evenings. We can manage to have our own rooms well ventilated. From home it is different.

The brain-worker, or the man who has been worried no matter how, will often find mental recreation in the concert-room, the theatre, or the lecture-hall. It cannot often be called healthful recreation, however, for the systems of ventilation in nearly all places of public resort are sadly in need of reform. And so from places of amusement, after breathing the vilest of atmospheres and the most obnoxious of gases, we return home, exhilarated in mind probably, but too often jaded and weary in body. Restless nights are the consequence, and, on the whole, we feel next day that it might have been better had we not indulged in such doubtful recreation.

Fashionable parties and balls cannot be said to combine the elements of healthful recreation, and yet they might do so, if it were not for the crime of over-crowding. In about a hundred years more or less this will doubtless be changed. Fashionable people will then prefer to give five "at homes" for one we give now, but comfort will be studied. We may fancy a *materfamilias* of these coming days reading with astonishment in some old novel of our over-crowded assemblies or ball-rooms, and remarking, " Well, poor creatures, I dare say they did it for economy's sake."

Now, dancing is to young people, and even to the middle-aged, a most exhilarating and healthful recreation where there is light and air and room to move, but dancing in an atmosphere laden with carbonic acid and over-heated is depressing in the extreme, and should be avoided as jading to the nerves, and productive of after fatigue.

But without doubt the best and most healthful recreation is that which combines exercise in the open air with amusement. It is this combination that makes out-door games so refreshingly recreative. While there are certainly not too many of these that men can indulge in, it is to be regretted there are so few in which women can engage. Lawn tennis is one grand and delightful exception, and as far as very young girls are concerned, I think cricket might well be another.

Women can skate in winter, and row in summer; both exercises are healthful, but both have a *sine quâ non*—water in one form or another.

One of the most healthful and exhilarating recreations I know is archery. For dear health's sake there ought to be an archery club in every parish. But alas! they are few and far between, and so girls must walk while their brothers are at play. Nevertheless, walking exercise is very far indeed from being despicable, but before it can be admitted into the category of healthful recreations, it must be of a sort to give pleasure to the person who engages in it. Walking should be always done in pleasant company; *the road should never seem long*, that is the real criterion by which we are to judge of the benefit likely to accrue from it.

Walking should never be done fast enough to make the heart beat rapidly or the breath come short, or the skin to be bathed in perspiration. If walking is to be done for health's sake, it must be really and truly a recreation, therefore I say, if you have a pleasant companion who is willing to undertake walking exercise with you, arrange for, not three or four walks, but thirty or forty, at the same time every day, rain or shine; and, if you can, combine with your strolling some such pleasant study as botany, geology, or some other branch of natural history.

The best form of exercise by far and away is tricycling.

On Growing Old.

First as to grey hair. This, taken alone, is by no means a sign of age either in the old or in the young. Many a fresh and youthful face I can call to mind, and so I have no doubt can you, which is topped by snowy hair. Some people get grey-haired when very young, and this peculiarity runs in families, and even in clans. It is generally, although not always, associated with the rheumatic or gouty diathesis, and the nervous temperament. And, as a rule, people who get early grey do not become bald. And, talking of grey hairs, I know a young lady of five-and-twenty who has, as our novelists would say, a wealth of wavy hair, and it hangs in beautiful rich ringlets, not of golden, but of silvery sheen. And I know the clergyman of a parish church, now in his ninety-third year, whose hair—his own hair, mind you—is still as black as the raven's wing.

The strength of an individual who has been a free and a fast liver decays at a very early age. But you cannot get such an one to believe that it is anything else except just the result of being a little out of sorts, which a few weeks at the seaside will be sure to put all right. Decay of the teeth is another sign of advancing age.

Loss of flesh and shrivelling is a much more serious symptom, and along with this, or as separate symptoms, you have breathlessness and perspiration on slight exertion, a general feeling of tiredness and *ennui*, and languor of the circulation.

Memory fails in the prematurely aged to a greater or less

extent, and conversational power, for the loss of which they endeavour to make up by telling anecdotes.

And now I've a word to say on wrinkles. Wrinkles look very nice in old people, but they do *not* become the young. The skin in age, whether young or old age, is not capable of fully performing its functions. It is not so pliant, it has become dry, and wrinkles easily.

Nothing, I think, shows age more surely than certain kinds of wrinkles. These generally are induced by fast living, which brings on dyspepsia and sluggish liver; these latter induce restless nights ; the skin about the eyes of a morning is slightly swollen and œdematous, and if this be continued for any length of time, it is easy to see how crow's-feet are permanently established. About the only class of wrinkles I care to see in the face of youth are those around the eyes, caused by smiling, that are signs of a merry heart which will never get old. Very different are those deep wrinkles that extend from each *ala* of the nose, and curve down the cheek towards the chin. These are most prominently seen in waiters, and in people engaged in business which necessitates their fawning on their customers. Such wrinkles are the result of smiles that are merely from the teeth forwards, and do not extend downwards to the heart or upwards to the eye. Avoid, therefore, smiling when you don't feel like it. *Esse quam videre* is a capital motto.

Avoid dyspepsia if you would live to a healthy old age. It causes sleeplessness, puffiness of the eyes, wrinkles, and grey hairs. Live plainly, and beware of highly-spiced made dishes and condiments of all kinds, and seek for an appetite in the fresh air. You cannot have too much of that. If you are temperate in eating, temperance in drinking will come naturally. Go in for daily and perfect ablution. Make this a regular habit. Do not neglect exercise. Never use any cosmetic for the face except rain-water, for one and all of them sooner or later injure the skin irremediably

Hard work, especially brain-work, must always be followed by a proportionate period of inactivity.

Avoid the use of stimulating oils for the hair. Occasional washing with the yolk of two or three eggs and rain-water, and the daily use of moderately hard brushes, are the great secrets of beautiful hair.

The use of a nicely-fitting corset is beneficial rather than otherwise, and although very tight lacing is injurious, medical men have had over-much to say about the matter. A well-made boot, too, can never injure anyone. Goodness forbid our English girls should ever be shaped like savages, either in feet or form! The customs of late hours and crowded rooms have a notoriously ageing influence on the youth of this country. They are the worms at the root of beauty's bloom, Now, young ladies, I do not for a moment meditate advising you to give up your balls and your parties. You *shall* dance and sing, and be generally jolly, for you are young, and if you didn't you would mope, and get ill and ugly; that would be worse, wouldn't it? Only take your pleasures moderately, and without too much excitement; and here is the best piece of advice I have given you yet: *Spend as much of the day as you can in out-door exercise*, so shall you enjoy your evening dance, and still be beautiful for ever. Lastly, do not wear too much clothing in summer, nor too little in winter; and never, if possible, lose your temper.

Do not think that there is no beauty in genuine old age, for, ah! indeed, indeed there is, if life has been well spent, just as there is beauty in the sunset of a long summer's day.

From a paper written by me last year for that most excellent magazine, "Young England," I cull the following. It contains one or two hints that may be of use to ladies and youths, for I must say that the former ride most rashly sometimes, and manifest a fine indifference to the rules of the road:

You will have chosen a machine with a good hand-brake; this, I believe, is the safest and best. But you must see that the drum beneath it, which it has to hold, be not too smooth or oily, else the brake may fail to act properly.

I was rushing downhill once at a speed of about twenty miles an hour, when I suddenly became cognisant of two terrible facts. One was that there was a precipice right ahead of me— a cliff it was—standing high over a stormy ocean, the other fact being that my brake would not bite, and I was, therefore, being whirled rapidly on to destruction. What did I do? What could I do? Why, I awoke in a fright. It was all owing to a lobster curry I had partaken of for supper. But, one may learn a lesson even in a dream.

Before starting on a ride, therefore, be perfectly sure that your brake is good.

Look, also, to every nut about the machine before you mount, for one getting loose and coming off might result in a painful accident.

You must not ride without a good bell, or "gong," as they are sometimes called, and this must be carefully kept from the wet when the machine is not in use. See also that your bell is well fastened on, or it may become useless during your journey.

For night riding you must have lamps. Do not buy the first you see in the market. Get a copy of *The Cyclist* before you buy your lamps. It will be a saving, for you will therein see advertisements of several excellent ones. The great fault with most of these lamps is that in riding over rough road the wick drops down into the oil, and the light goes out. This on a dark night would be a disagreeable *contretemps*.

Now a brief line or two as regards what I call pastime studies.

I should like very much to have support in carrying out an idea I have for some time had in head, if not also in hand. This idea is the formation of a club, or rather a society of cyclists, the members of which, instead of rushing insanely and blindly from place to place, manufacturing records, and injuring their health, would ride in reason, with open mental and bodily eyes, and take notes of all they see and learn. Different branches of this society would take different subjects, and study these in the districts they tour in.

Thus we would, or will, have our botanists, our antiquaries, our geologists, our ancient historians, our

G

students of character and scenery, our fishermen, our photographers, and our artists.

In this last sentence there are embodied the names of a few of the pursuits I think those travelling by cycle for health and rational enjoyment should take up.

As to photography, good hints are given in Messrs. Iliffe and Son's work " Tricycling for Ladies."

Let me give just one concluding hint on the subject of pastime studies. Before starting on a tour the rider ought to read up his subject, so as to be perfectly at home in it, and before settling down in any district for a month or two, he or she ought to get from local publishers books bearing on the ancient history of the country.

Guide-books are fairly reliable, but there are many larger works about every place of historical interest that are far better than these.

CHAPTER XIV.

FISHING: A PASTIME FOR THE SUMMER HOLIDAY.—
CONCLUDING ADVICE.

BEING passionately fond of the sport of fishing myself, I think I cannot err by devoting a few of my concluding pages to the subject, by way of recommending it to my cycling readers as a pastime eminently suitable for those who desire to get as much good from the summer holiday as possible.

The question may be asked by many: Is fishing a sport suitable for the fair sex?

I answer, unhesitatingly, "Yes," and I consider it eminently so.

Away up in the Scottish Highlands I have known many brave young girls who have gone to the hill in the grouse season, riding part of the way, perhaps, on ponies, then going on all day on foot through the heather and over the hills, and bringing down their birds to the evident admiration, not only of the ghillies and keepers, but of the dogs themselves. Healthful and all as this may be, I cannot recommend it to many ladies. Indeed, only those with extra fine physique could endure the fatigue.

But fishing is quite another thing.

I must be understood to refer to three kinds of fishing only, for this simple reason—I have not been experienced in any other. As for bottom fishing, I do not care for it. Carp fishing is fairly good, but the fish himself is not a gastronomic dainty. Dutchmen, they say, keep the poor fellow hung up in a basket of damp moss for a few weeks, cramming him every day with bread soaked in milk, and he then loses the flavour of mud for which he is celebrated. This is not treating the carp well. It is adding insult to injury, and cruelty to that.

The three kinds of fishing recommend for those in search of health, or those who want to regenerate after months of hard work, toil and moil, and worry, are—

I. Angling in a stream in a pleasant, healthy, bracing country place, especially in Scotland.

II. Angling in lochs (Scotch), or English and Welsh tarns and lakes.

III. Fishing on the sea.

Apart from cycling itself—an exercise which, as I have taken occasion to hint, is often overdone—there is no more wholesome recreation than that of fishing in streams and in rivers. Even in Scotland I much prefer the streamlet or burn to the river itself. I have never much, if any, difficulty in obtaining fishing in salmon rivers, but, strange though it may seem, I have a partiality for trout-fishing. I may fish for salmon all day, and, though I flatter myself I know how to make a decent cast, be like the Apostle Peter and catch nothing. On the other hand, if the day be anything like what is wanted, from a burn I can generally manage to make a basket of trout. Those streamlets that run into or out of lakes, or those that join rivers are the best, and away in the

Scottish, and perhaps in the Welsh Highlands, one can usually fall in with some hop-o'-my-thumb of a village urchin to do duty as ghillie. These little chaps often know better where to go than his lordship's keeper himself, so their acquaintance is worth cultivating.

At most of the hotels in the villages of the North, say up Donside or Deeside, if you live in the hotel you can have fishing free.

The same may be said of fishing in lakes or lochs, if the hotel is anywhere near it. Take Dalwhinnie, for example, which is close to the great Loch Ericht, under the shadow of mountains nearly a mile high above the sea-level, and on whose tops the snow never melts. The fishing on this wondrous loch is splendid. The mountain air is exceedingly bracing, so much so that I would not advise anyone, unless very strong indeed, to go fishing in a boat without taking something to eat and drink in the bag. And if there be anyone that knows better than another how to make a nice sandwich it is Mrs. McDonald, the kindly Lady of the Lake who presides over this mountain hostelry.

About fishing from boats on the sea, I need not say much. Most of this branch of the art piscatorial that l have followed has been in the lone Hebrides; but in good evenings the sport is splendid.

Here, again, a ghillie will be found handy for either ady or gentlemen. He will carry a creel of fish as heavy as himself—more or less. He will guide you to the best spots and bays amongst the rocks, he will busk your hooks and bait your lines, and for a few bawbees be as faithful to you as the Dougal Craytur was to Helen McGregor.

All over Inverness-shire and Ross, and the North of Scotland generally, fishing is not difficult to obtain. I do not say that you will be able always to make big bags, for, though some do not think so, there is an art in fishing which ought to be learned young; but I do say that the pastime tends to calm the nervous system, purify the blood, and rest and strengthen a weary, worn-out frame.

Try it!

In the border-country fishing is sometimes a little difficult to get; but, after all, difficulties are just like ninepins—they were made to be knocked over.

I shall now mention a few of the streams in this territory, leaving to the cycling angler's own tact and judgment the getting of permission to cast a fly or sink a worm therein:—

1.—The Aln: Part free; some good sport—trout.

2.—The Coquet: *The* best river in Northumbria—trout; excellent sport; delightful scenery. Also in small tributaries.

3.—The Wansbeck: Free about Morpeth only, or free by paying a small sum. Application to proprietors sure to meet with a hospitable response.

4.—The Font: A tributary of the Wansbeck. Same remarks apply to it.

5.—The Tyne, Wark Burn, Keilder, and Blyth: All fairly good. Rather restricted.

6.—The Tweed: The best of salmon rivers. The best

hint I can give is this—buy your tackle from the makers who are in business in the towns near this river and its tributaries, and ask for advice, which, when found, make a note of.

7.—The Teviot: *Very* good for angling, especially at lower end. License 5s., obtainable at Hawick. Ask the postmaster.

8.—The Jed : Fairly good.

9.—The Ettrick : Good.

10.—The Leader and its tributary, the Earnscleugh : Good for trout, and, I believe, nearly all open to the angler.

11.—The Till : Very good, and in many parts free.

12.—The Glen, a tributary of Till : Capita .

13.—The Whitadder and Blackadder and Eye all afford varied and excellent sport for the enthusiastic fisherman.

A civil letter to the postmaster of any town on the banks of any of the streams mentioned, if it enclosed a stamped addressed envelope, would secure you a civil reply. Before going to strange towns I have frequently adopted this plan, asking for the address of a quiet and good hotel, temperance or otherwise. Once settled there, I never found much difficulty in getting fairly good sport.

And now, as in a small work like the present it is quite as great a fault in the author to say too much as too little, it is time, I think, for me to retire. I bid my cycling friends once more adieu, and from the bottom of my heart I wish them that greatest of all earthly blessings, HEALTH.

ADVERTISEMENT PREFACE.

THIS is to Certify that all Goods, &c., advertised in this book can be depended upon as genuine. No Advertisement has been solicited or accepted from anyone, or any firm, whose articles I cannot *well* recommend.

W. GORDON STABLES,

C.M., M.D., R.N.

www.ingramcontent.com/pod-product-compliance
Lightning Source LLC
Chambersburg PA
CBHW022147160426
43197CB00009B/1457